1996

ANALYSIS
OF
THE
INDIVIDUAL

ANALYSIS
OF
THE
INDIVIDUAL

Marjory Brown-Azarowicz

Nelson-Hall
nh Chicago

LIBRARY OF CONGRESS CATALOGING IN PUBLICATION DATA

Brown-Azarowicz, Marjory Frances.
    Analysis of the individual.

        Bibliography: p.
        Includes index.
        1. Counseling—Methodology.   2.   Personality tests.
I. Title.
BF637.C6B765   1985   158 # .3   85–8803
ISBN 0–8304–1029–5

Manufactured in the United States of America

10   9   8   7   6   5   4   3   2   1

The paper in this book is pH neutral (acid-free).

Dedicated to Diane, Michael, Calvin, and Debby

CONTENTS

PREFACE

This book is designed as a text in the analysis of clients' problems for counselors in elementary and secondary education, and higher education, and those involved in family counseling, career counseling, counseling those with emotional and criminal problems, and counseling the elderly. It is based upon five years of class work with graduate students who helped develop the content, questionnaires, and basic premises. It is believed that counselors who understand themselves will be better able to understand and help clients analyze and solve problems. Thus, emphasis is placed upon the counselor's self-awareness (chapter 2, Counselor, Know Thyself). Section 2, Analyzing Data, utilizes the steps in the interview and case study to develop each aspect of analysis. The selection of data, (chapter 4) is based upon wise decision making. The analysis of data (chapter 5) is based upon a sound knowledge of what tests really mean and the cautions that must be exercised in helping clients choose problem solutions that are best for them. This section includes detailed steps for the development of an interview (chapter 2), the case study and case conference (chapter 3), and concludes with chapter 6, about writing techniques for appraisal reports.

Section 3, Methods and Materials, has chapters on the usage of non-test techniques (chapters 7, 8, and 9) for each type of counseling setting. Included are self-reporting devices, staff reports, and sociometric scales. Chapters 10 and 11 discuss models of counseling. This section closes with a chapter on the ethical standards of professional organizations and legal considerations for the counselor.

Section 4 presents role-playing parts for students' practice. These cases are supplemented throughout the book by role-playing sections related to interviews, case conferences, and the selection and analysis of data.

For the past eighty years, an extensive technical, psychological, and statistical knowledge about testing human abilities has been developed. This knowledge must be summarized succinctly by counselors if they are to help clients identify, analyze, and solve the problems that cause them to function poorly in their private and social lives. To do so, the counselor must have a knowledge of the tests and techniques pertinent to clients' problems. The counselor must be able to collect viable data and then sift, analyze, reject, or utilize materials gathered about a client in order to work with those materials that will lead to problem solution. This complex process is one that entails personal understandings, technical knowledge, and the wisdom to choose the data, materials, and counseling techniques that are likely to help a particular client solve his or her problems.

For the client, problem solution is dependent upon personal resources plus the counselor's wise usage of tests and techniques in analysis. The counselor's ability is dependent upon much experience with similar problems in practical as well as simulated settings. Counselors who have this knowledge and experience are likely to make wise decisions that will help in problem solution.

Today, much emphasis is placed upon the need for high ethical standards in counseling others. Federal legislation demands accountability in counseling decisions and actions. These laws and regulations make it imperative that competency in all aspects of analysis is maintained.

This text is based upon the belief that individuals who wish to become counselors in schools and colleges, in family and career centers, to the elderly, and to those with emotional and criminal problems, need to be able to:

- analyze data in ways that enhance the solution of clients' problems
- analyze data with clear understanding of the meanings, cautions, and uses of standardized and nonstandardized tests and non-test techniques
- understand themselves as persons so that personal biases and prejudices will not hamper the processes of analysis and problem solution
- have a pragmatic knowledge of the uses of non-test techniques in each type of counseling setting
- have had experiences in problem solving through the role playing of interviews and case conferences
- have a knowledge of the ways in which data are gathered for case studies
- write easily understood appraisal reports
- comprehend the models of counseling applicable to the counselor's own field of counseling

- understand the types of transactions, games, and roles that may be played by clients and counselors in counseling
- know the basic legal and ethical implications of laws and professional standards that apply to counseling
- develop wisdom in the application of the learnings stated above through many experiences in role playing.

SECTION ONE

INTRODUCTION

CHAPTER ONE

Counselor, Know Thyself

To know oneself in aspects of life and personality that may affect the counselor-client relationship is a necessity if analyses of individuals are to be objective and effective. Each counselor brings to the profession a lifetime of beliefs, attitudes, and prejudices about others that may affect the counseling relationship. During college years and the living and work experiences of life, each individual is exposed to experiences with many groups of people. These experiences cause reevaluation of personal attitudes. For counselors, personal reevaluation is a continuing professional necessity. Counseling brings one in contact with clients at critical times in their lives. The counselor must be able to help these individuals without undue personal bias. A counselor should grow in wisdom and understanding of people and their problems and of personal attitudes toward these individuals. The counselor must have the ability to believe in the worthiness of others. He or she has to be able to view the individual as a unique being capable of adjustment and wise decision-making in personal problem solving. Each client is involved in a unique environmental setting with which he/she must come to terms. The counselor's preconceived ideas of how this is to be accomplished do not have a place in counseling. Therefore, the counselor must bring to the counseling setting a knowledge of how personal beliefs affect actions toward clients.

There are basic standards upon which a community operates, such as obedience to laws, work ethics, nurture and care of the young and old, and honesty in individual and group relationships. Within this cultural-community framework of standards, the client must learn to solve personal problems. Counselors may guide and make suggestions, but the client is responsible for all decisions. Adjustment to society in personal areas of life is the province of the client. This means that the counselor must understand problems through the eyes of the client, the client's community, and the total society. The counselor's personal attitudes, biases, and prejudices should not be interjected into the decision-making process. The counselor must learn to be acutely conscious of areas of personal subjectivity. Without this ability to see oneself as one really is, the counselor's ability as a helping person is negated.

The process of self-realization is humbling, because it shows the counselor the realities of his or her personal attitudes. It also helps the counselor to think objectively and to understand the times when personal subjectivity is intruding upon analysis. When the counselor does not realize that personal subjectivity is intruding upon analysis, the counselor-client relationship is dangerous for the client. The client may be removed from personal decision-making and decisions may be based upon the counselor's value system rather than the client's. How does a counselor go about self-understanding? For individuals reared in open-communicative family styles, self-understanding is part of life.

For those reared in closed, less open-to-society family styles, definite steps should be taken. For many counselors, self-understanding is a true need. Some individuals with strong interpersonal biases do not have a place in the counseling profession. Counseling attracts many persons from closed-family styles who wish to help others. As idealistic as these individuals may be, they enter the counseling profession with a set of liabilities. These liabilities can only impede counselor-client effectiveness, unless the counselors have an accurate perspective of their own personalities. They must be willing to completely change unfavorable attitudes. If their previous life styles have not considered self-understanding as a value to be sought, "knowing oneself" may be a very painful process. For some individuals, it may prove to be an impossible task.

For the counselor already in the profession, continued self-understanding is helpful in order to meet the pressures of the job with equanimity. In counseling, one must learn to work with much negative feedback to one's ego. The emotional impact over a period of time is dependent upon one's inner resources, one's ability to be optimistic and cheerful within oneself, and one's ability to develop a life style that compensates for the emotional drainage of varied counseling positions. A wise counselor knows his or her personal weaknesses, biases, and attitudes toward others and is willing to improve the objectivity of interpersonal relationships. This may be done by developing a scientific, objective approach to problems, clients, and the pressures of the profession.

Steps toward Self-Understanding

The steps a counselor may take toward self-understanding are gradual and should continue throughout one's lifetime. A first step is a desire to know oneself. To understand oneself, as a counselor, does not mean to enter into therapy. If this is needed, the counselor should avoid counseling others until personal problems are settled. Clients need sound, well-adjusted counselors if they are to be helped effectively. Short-term crisis therapy is a different matter, but long-term personality-type therapies usually signal trouble for counselor-client relationships.

A useful second step is to take a personality test such as the Minnesota Multiphasic Personality Inventory. Note if one's profile lies within one standard deviation above or below the norm for one's age, sex, and range of occupation. These are normal ranges, but scores that are two or three standard deviations from the norm should be considered carefully. Are these deviations with which you agree? If you agree, would these deviations harm the counselor-client relationship? If so, what will you do about them? If you do not agree, take another personality test and reassess your scores.

A third step is to listen to friends' and relatives' opinions about your personality traits. In families, we tend to live up to family beliefs about our personalities. Question your reactions to these beliefs. Are they true? How much do these beliefs affect you as a person? Re-evaluate your values and biases as related to your family/parental values as follows:

1. List in two columns the values you (1) admire and (2) do not admire in your parents' or family's life style.
2. List in two columns the prejudices, biases, and values you (1) admire and (2) do not admire in your present life style.
3. List in two columns the factors in your present life style that will (1) help and (2) hinder clients in problem solution.

A fourth step is to work or live within communities about which you are biased or in which you intend to counsel but lack experience. This is a difficult, yet important step for a counselor to take. Without this step, one's effectiveness as a counselor will be minimized. This procedure should cause one to mature and develop positively as a counselor. However, it may cause one to be more prejudiced than before. Your attitude and reasons for the living arrangements are the key. The chance to live in a differing community is a chance to become acquainted with oneself. One may ask, ''How do I react to the differences? How do I feel about myself when community values are different? What is of value within this community? How may I learn to react positively? Within this life style, are there values I wish I had in my life style?''

A fifth step is to assess oneself using the Reactions Questionnaire that follows. Counselor-client relationships are influenced by the counselor's reactions toward education, social levels, minorities, male-female roles, religion, politics, and interpersonal relationships. All aspects of problem solving are affected, including the ways in which a problem will be studied, the analysis of data, and the suggested solutions. The Reactions Questionnaire will help you, as a counselor, to assess your personal attitudes toward others. Be honest with yourself and try to assess your true feelings. Use the Reactions Questionnaire Answer Sheet. Check the squares with your choice of (a) naturally easy, (b) can bring myself to do it, or (c) very difficult. When all questions are answered, total each column on the answer sheet.

Reactions Questionnaire

From your point of view, how easy would it be for you to:	(Check one)		
	a. Naturally easy	b. Can bring myself to do it	c. Very difficult

I. *Education*
1. Study long hours
2. Spend vacations in scholarly pursuits rather than on holiday
3. Give up a lucrative job in exchange for a long-term educational pursuit
4. Spend a higher percentage of family income on books and education than on food
5. Try to persuade someone to obtain an education
6. Frequently utilize the services of your public library
7. Go to college for extra course work
8. Encourage the most brilliant person you know
9. Attend a meeting of persons with IQs above 160
10. Have an uneducated person as a best friend
11. Live with people who do not care to educate themselves or their children above minimal levels
12. Accept the fact that your scholarship is not high enough for you to be accepted into the honor society of your discipline
13. Be accepted as a member of Who's Who among graduate students

II. *Social Levels*
1. Have the richest person you know as best friend
2. Be accepted into the most distinguished country club in your community

	(Check one)		
From your point of view, how easy would it be for you to:	a. Naturally easy	b. Can bring myself to do it	c. Very difficult

    3. Attend a dinner at the White House
    4. Date a person far above your social level
    5. Marry into a family of wealth
    6. Have the economically poorest person you know as best friend
    7. Be accepted as an equal by a family with a very low income
    8. Eat dinner in an urban slum home
    9. Marry a person whose father is a day laborer
   10. Date a person so far below your social stratum that your family/friends complain
   11. Be a janitor
   12. Give a poor family food and clothing
   13. Give 10 percent of your income, regularly, to charity

III. *Differing Cultures*
    1. Comb a black person's hair
    2. Comb a white person's hair
    3. Shake hands with a white person
    4. Shake hands with a black person
    5. Hold hands with a white person
    6. Hold hands with a black person
    7. Kiss a black person
    8. Kiss a white person
    9. Go to a picnic where everyone speaks a language you do not understand
   10. Live in a foreign country
   11. Work with people not of your own race

From your point of view, how easy would it be for you to:	(Check one)		
	a. Naturally easy	b. Can bring myself to do it	c. Very difficult

    12. Live in a neighborhood in which you are the only person of your ethnic origin

    13. Accept your child's marriage to someone of a differing racial origin

IV. *The Handicapped*

    1. Hug a person with severe facial disfigurement

    2. Kiss a person with a severe facial disfigurement

    3. Keep up a conversation with a person who is subnormal in intelligence

    4. Live in a home where one adult is emotionally unstable and dangerous to others

    5. Marry a handicapped person

    6. Have a handicapped person for your best friend

    7. Make your vocation one in which you serve only handicapped persons

    8. Accept the finality of a severe handicap to yourself that was brought on by disease or an accident

    9. Accept a severe handicap to a loved one brought on by disease or an accident

    10. Show no change of facial expression when you see a severely disfigured person

    11. Tell people you meet socially or at work about a close relative with an hereditary handicap

    12. Take your severely handicapped child to an institution for total lifetime care

	(Check one)		
From your point of view, how easy would it be for you to:	a. Naturally easy	b. Can bring myself to do it	c. Very difficult

    13. Live in a household with disabled persons

V. *The Elderly*

    1. Look after elderly people as a vocation

    2. Take care of an ambulatory elderly relative

    3. Scream at an elderly person

    4. Be annoyed by an elderly person's slowed physical and mental reactions

    5. Miss a social appointment while taking an elderly person shopping

    6. Become a regular volunteer for Meals-On-Wheels for the elderly

    7. Accept the inevitable declining physical and mental strength of a loved elderly relative

    8. Listen to an aged person talk about his/her ailments

    9. Choose to go to the beach with two elderly persons on Memorial Day rather than to go out with your own age group

    10. Keep up a conversation with an aged person

    11. Place a parent in a nursing home

    12. Cheerfully accept the finality of a nursing home when you are old

    13. Accept yourself, when eighty years of age, as a person with weakening physical and mental powers

	(Check one)		
From your point of view, how easy would it be for you to:	a. Naturally easy	b. Can bring myself to do it	c. Very difficult

VI. *Male-Female Relationships*
  1. Wear clothing used traditionally by persons of the opposite sex
  2. Engage in athletic activities traditionally done by persons of the opposite sex, e.g., football for women, ballet for men
  3. (If a male) be sweet, shy, and retiring in a business or professional setting OR (if a female) be aggressive, loud, and demanding in a business or professional setting
  4. Wash dishes every day
  5. Make your bed every day
  6. Scrub your kitchen floor each week
  7. Take out the garbage
  8. Change a tire on your car
  9. Fix a broken electric switch
  10. Pay for the dinner of a person of the opposite sex
  11. Clean a baby's diaper
  12. Go to a homosexual picnic
  13. Accept a woman as priest, minister, or rabbi in your church or synagogue

VII. *Religious-Political Attitudes*
  1. Take part in a picket line or demonstration about a political cause in which you believe
  2. Write a letter to your Congressman about a political matter of importance
  3. Run for an elected position in local government

			(Check one)		
From your point of view, how easy would it be for you to:		a. Naturally easy	b. Can bring myself to do it	c. Very difficult	

4. Take a petition to your neighbors about a political cause
5. Vote in an election .
6. Be active in a political party
7. Go to a constituency meeting of your church or synagogue and speak against a current practice which you believe is harmful
8. Read the religious literature of a church or synagogue not of your own beliefs
9. Become a member of another religious denomination
10. Never attend church or synagogue or read religious literature
11. Converse without anger with a religious person who is trying to force his/her ideas upon you
12. Go to court for an atheist who is being discriminated against in his or her place of employment for his or her beliefs
13. Go to court for a person of another religious faith who is being discriminated against in his or her place of employment for his or her religious beliefs

VIII. *Personal Reactions to Others*
1. Accept unjust criticism about your work
2. See the positive side of a person who does not like you

From your point of view, how easy would it be for you to:	a. Naturally easy	b. Can bring myself to do it	c. Very difficult
		(Check one)	
3. Refrain from telling a person what you think of his or her actions after he or she has told others an untrue story about you			
4. Work with someone you do not like			
5. Be kind to someone who has maliciously wronged you			
6. Drive at or below the speed limit			
7. Abide by the honor code of your university and never cheat during an exam			
8. Find and make amends to the person whose car fender you have dented in the parking lot			
9. Look objectively at a story told by the family gossip			
10. Console a bereaved person			
11. Be kind to others when you are ill			
12. Refrain from feeling superior to classmates who make lower grades than you			
13. At a busy intersection, go back and help a person who has fallen and is injured			

Reactions Questionnaire Answer Sheet

This answer sheet is divided into eight sections that correspond to the eight sections in the Reactions Questionnaire: I Education (ED); II Social Levels (SOC); III Differing Cultures (DIC); IV The Handicapped (HAN); V The Elderly (ELD); VI Male-Female Relationships (M–F); VII Religious-Political Attitudes (R–P); and VIII Personal Reactions to Others (OTH).

Directions: Fill in the boxes with your choice of (a) naturally easy, (b) can bring myself to do it, and (c) very difficult

Questions	I ED			II SOC			III DIC			IV HAN			V ELD			VI M–F			VII R–P			VIII O
	a	b	c	a	b	c	a	b	c	a	b	c	a	b	c	a	b	c	a	b	c	a
1																						
2																						
3																						
4																						
5																						
6																						
7																						
8																						
9																						
10																						
11																						
12																						
13																						
Totals																						

Scoring the Reactions Questionnaire

There are no right or wrong answers to the Reactions Questionnaire. The questionnaire presents a profile of an individual's reactions to the items in the eight categories. The "a" scores show easy reactions to an item, while the "c" scores show difficulty. Note the categories in which "c" scores predominate. Assess personal reasons for these "c" scores. Decide what you intend to do with your attitudes and reactions as you pursue a counseling career.

Further analyses of parts of each category are listed below. For individuals with few "a" scores, the following section should be read carefully.

Scoring Parts of Categories

The eight categories and parts of these categories will help individuals assess their reactions to the following questions. Answers are found by noting on the individual's answer sheet the items listed after each question.

I. *Education*
   A. How do you relate to persons who have varying academic and intellectual abilities and pursuits? Note category I, items 1–13.
   B. How committed to intellectual pursuits is your life style? Note category I, items 1–7.
   C. How do you relate to those who have a good education? Note category I, items 8 and 9.
   D. How do you relate to those who do not have a good education? Note category I, items 10 and 11.
   E. How do you accept your intellectual strengths and weaknesses? Note category I, items 12 and 13.

II. *Social Levels*
   A. How do you react to persons of differing social levels? Note category II, items 1–13.
   B. How do you react to those who are high on the social scale? Note category II, items 1–5.
   C. How do you react to those who are considered lower than you socially? Note category II, items 6–11.

D. How easy is it for you to become involved with helping the poor? Note category II, items 12 and 13.

III. *Differing Cultures*
A. How do you react to persons of differing cultures? Note category III, items 1–13.
B. Toward which of the following groups do you have prejudices?

> Whites: category III, items 2,3,5, and 8
> Blacks: category III, items 1,4,6, and 7

C. How easy is it for you to relate to persons with differing racial and ethnic backgrounds? Note category III, items 9–13.

IV. *The Handicapped*
How do you relate to the handicapped? Note category IV, items 1–13.

V. *The Elderly*
A. How easily do you accept elderly people? Note category V, items 1–13.
B. What do you believe will be your acceptance of yourself as an elderly person? Note category V, items 12 and 13.

VI. *Male-Female Relationships*
A. How easily do you accept men and women as equals? Note category VI, items 1–13.
B. How easily do you accept yourself without stereotyped sex roles? Note category VI, items 1–12.

VII. *Religious-Political Attitudes*
A. In which area, religious or political, are your reactions difficult?

> Political: category VII, items 1–6
> Religious: category VII, items 7–13

B. In which area, religious or political, would you be willing to help others?

> Political: category VII, items 1,2,4, and 6
> Religious: category VII, items 7,12, and 13

VIII. *Personal Reactions to Others*
A. How do you react toward persons who have wronged you or whom you do not like? Note category VIII, items 1–5.
B. Is it easy for you to abide by practised or written community rules relating to others? Note category VIII, items 6–8.

C. How do you react to others in situations where there is nothing tangible in the relationship for you? Note category VIII, items 9–13.

List of Personality Tests

Some personality tests that will prove useful in your self-assessment are:

Bell Adjustment Inventory for adults has scores for home, occupational, health, social, and emotional. (Hugh M. Bell, Consulting Psychologists Press, Inc.)

The California Psychological Inventory for ages 13-plus has scores for dominance, sociability, social presence, self-acceptance, sense of well-being, responsibility, socialization, self-control, tolerance, good impression, communality, achievement via conformance, achievement via independence, intellectual efficiency, psychological mindedness, flexibility, and femininity. (Harrison G. Gough, Consulting Psychologists Press, Inc.)

California Test of Personality for adults has scores for self-reliance, sense of personal worth, sense of personal freedom, feeling of belonging, withdrawing tendencies, nervous systems, total personal adjustment, social standards, social skills, antisocial tendencies, family relations, occupational relations, and community relations. (Louis P. Thorpe, Willis W. Clark, and Ernest W. Tiegs, California Test Bureau.)

D.F. Opinion Survey for college age and adults has scores for need for attention, desire for thinking, adventure vs. security, self-reliance vs. dependence, aesthetic appreciation, cultural conformity, need for freedom, realistic thinking, need for precision, and need for diversion. (J. P. Guilford, Paul R. Christensen, and Nicholas A. Bond, Sheridan Psychological Services, Inc.)

Edwards Personal Preference Schedule for college age and adults has scores for achievement, deference, order, exhibition, autonomy, affiliation, succorance, dominance, abasement, nurturance, change, endurance, heterosexuality, and aggression. (Allen L. Edwards, Psychological Corporation.)

Edwards Personality Inventory for adults has 53 scores in four booklets. (Allen L. Edwards, Science Research Associates.)

FIRO (Fundamental Interpersonal Relations Orientation) *Scales* for adults consist of tests on FIRO behavior, FIRO feelings, life interpersonal history inquiry, marital attitudes evaluation, and educational values. (William C. Schultz, Consulting Psychologists Press, Inc.)

Guilford-Zimmerman Temperament Survey for adults has scores for general activity, restraint, ascendance, sociability, emotional stability, objectivity, friendliness, thoughtfulness, personal relations, and masculinity. (J. P. Guilford and Wayne S. Zimmerman, Sheridan Psychological Services, Inc.)

Kuder Preference Record—Personal for adults has scores for group activity, stable situations, working with ideas, avoiding conflict, directing others, and verification. (G. Frederic Kuder, Science Research Associates.)

Minnesota Multiphasic Personality Inventory for adults has scores for hypochondriasis, depression, hysteria, psychopathic deviation, masculinity and femininity, paranoia, psychasthenia, hypomania, schizophrenia, and social. (Starke R. Hathaway and J. C. McKinley, Psychological Corporation.)

The Personal Audit for adults has scores for emotional adjustment, seriousness, firmness, frankness, tranquility, stability, tolerance, steadiness, persistence, and contentment. (Clifford R. Adams and William L. Lepley, Science Research Associates.)

Personality Inventory (Benreuter) for adults has scores for neurotic tendency, self-sufficiency, introversion-extroversion, dominance-submission, confidence, and sociability. (Robert G. Benreuter, Consulting–Psychological Press, Inc.)

Rutgers Social Attribute Inventory for adults has fourteen trait ratings of perception of others as either real persons or generalized classes. (William D. Wells, Psychometric Affiliates.)

Scale to Measure Attitudes toward Disabled Persons (H. A. Yuker, J. R. Block, and J. A. Young, Human Resources Center.)

Sixteen Personality Factors Questionnaire for ages sixteen-plus has scores for reserved vs. outgoing, less intelligent vs. more intelligent, affected by feelings vs. emotionally stable, humble vs. assertive, sober vs. happy-go-lucky, expedient vs. conscientious, shy vs. venturesome, tough-minded vs. tender-minded, trusting vs. suspicious, practical vs. imaginative, forthright vs. shrewd, self-assured vs. apprehensive, conservative vs. experimenting, group dependent vs. self-sufficient, undisciplined vs. disciplined, self conflict vs. controlled, and relaxed vs. tense. (Raymond B. Cattell and H. W. Eber, Institute for Personality and Ability Testing.)

Social Intelligence Test: George Washington University Series for adults has scores for judgment in social situations, recognition of the mental state of speaker, memory for names and faces, observation of human behavior, and sense of humor. (F. A. Moss, T. Hunt, K. T. Omwake, and L. G. Woodward, Center for Psychological Service.)

Study of Values: A Scale for Measuring the Dominant Interests in Personality for adults has scores for theoretical, economic, aesthetic, social, political, and religious. (G. W. Allport, P. E. Vernon, and G. Lindzey, Houghton Mifflin.)

Thorndike Dimensions of Temperament for adults has scores for cheerful, placid, accepting, tough-minded, reflective, impulsive, active, and responsible. (Robert L. Thorndike, Psychological Corp.)

Thurstone Temperament Scale for adults has scores for active, vigorous, impulsive, dominant, stable, sociable, and reflective. (L. L. Thurstone, Science Research Associates.)

Vineland Social Maturity Scale used from birth to maturity, has 117 items separated into age groups that measure the actual and customary behavior of the individual. (Edgar A. Doll, American Guidance Service Inc.)

Bibliography

Buros, Oscar K., ed. *Personality Tests and Reviews.* Highland Park, N.J., Gryphon Press, 1970.

Woods, Robert H., ed. *Encylopedia of Clinical Assessment.* Vols. 1 and 2. Washington: Jossey-Bass, 1980.

SECTION TWO

ANALYZING

DATA

CHAPTER TWO

The Interview

The interview is a major technique in the counseling procedure and is an interpersonal, verbal communication process in which the prime objective is problem solution. The interview may be a one-time technique or it may be an ongoing technique used over a long period of time. By means of the interview, the counselor may discover the client's background, perception of problems, needs and desires, communication skills, personal factors that may inhibit problem solution, and problem-solving skills. For optimum service to the client, the interview should be conducted in a professional manner in an atmosphere of mutual trust, with the solution of the client's problems as the foremost objective. This chapter contains a variety of interviewing techniques and will present ideas for practising and analyzing abilities in the use of these techniques.

Interviews may be prepared or unprepared. Unprepared interviews are the most common and are usually initial interviews in which the counselor knows little or nothing about the client. Clients seek help in a counseling center because they believe the services offered may meet their needs. In the initial interview, the counselor may be able to obtain background information about the client by means of questionnaires or a discussion. She or he may discover major problem areas and can outline the resources available to the client within the counseling center.

Prepared Interviews

Preparation

Before an interview, pertinent data about the client should be re-viewed. These may be notes from previous interviews, anecdotal and observational records, questionnaires, and the results of standardized and nonstandardized tests. The purposes, desired objectives, and over-all format of the interview should be stated clearly. Depending upon the setting, the desired objectives might be to "find out why Mary, in grade seven, is failing math," "discover why Jack, age eleven, is afraid of his parents," "help Mrs. Jones realize that she can cope with the de-mands of a large family," or "aid Mr. Green in finding a job." The overall format should list key questions that will be answered during the interview. A time frame should be included so that the interview may be completed in the allotted time. The counselor should understand that a highly preplanned structure may prevent the free flow of ideas that leads to problem solution. However, some type of structure is needed to keep the interview on course and to guide discussion when communication breaks down. Thus, preplanning should be a blend of structure and openness to the development of ideas in problem solu-tion. An example of the preplanning needed for an interview follows. Mrs. Williams, forty-five, divorced, is living on welfare but wants to be self-supporting. She is unable to work at many jobs because she has asthma and is allergic to many things. She has just completed her high school diploma through night school and wants to know how she can gain more education in order to earn a living.

Purpose: To help Mrs. Williams reach decisions about ways in which she may gain more education in order to earn a living.

Strategy Questions:
1. In your aptitude tests, what were your best academic areas?
2. In which jobs are your allergies a handicap?
3. In which jobs are your academic weaknesses a handicap?
4. How will your education be financed?
5. Will you be able to complete your studies and work at a job with your allergies?

Time frame: 35 minutes
 5 minutes: review and state problem
20 minutes: discussion to answer questions
10 minutes: review, summary, and referrals.

Beginning the Interview

Physical Setting

The physical setting should be conducive to communication. Chairs and tables should be arranged to maximize conversation. Pictures, lamps, and objects should convey the purposes of the center or agency. For example, a job placement agency may look like a business office, whereas a women's crisis center may have a homelike appearance.

The Introduction

"A convenient time, a private space, a friendly smile and a courteous, businesslike manner will go a long way toward making an interview successful."[1] Begin with a few generalized remarks that will enable the client to relax and feel that this is a friendly place to be. "Be positive in attitude. If the client is hostile or frightened, ease fears and show that your prime objective is to help."[2] After the initial greetings, state what you believe to be the purposes for the interview. Then ask the client to verbalize the purposes or the problems. Both parties in an interview, client and counselor, must have the same clearly defined purposes. Otherwise, misunderstandings arise and the purposes of the interview may be negated.

The Discussion

The aim of the discussion section of an interview is to solve problems. During the discussion, the counselor must keep this aim clearly in mind. Attention may be focused upon problem solution by helping the client state facts, noting ways in which problems may be solved, and developing long- and short-term goals. The counselor should have in mind a tentative interview format, time frame, and prepared questions. The counselor must realize that although one interview will not solve a long-term problem, smaller problems may be solved and the solutions to long-term problems begun. The discussion may be directive, nondirective, or a combination.

This chapter discusses a structured interview in which preplanned questions are used to keep the discussion focused on problem solution.

Discussion Formats

Discussion formats should change and develop throughout an interview. Adequate preparation insures a productive discussion. However, the counselor may utilize any format or method that will help the client toward problem solution.

One format the counselor may use is to follow, in detail, preplanned strategies and questions, encouraging the client to elaborate on these and to develop tangents of thought. However, the discussion should return to agreed-upon purposes and point toward solutions to the client's problems. Within this structure, the counselor may use directive or nondirective approaches.

A free-flowing format that does not have preplanned questions or defined goals may be utilized in settings where the client is unable to move toward problem solution. The client may need to talk to an interested person, develop thought patterns, explore feelings, and place ideas in a free nonjudgmental communicative environment. If these discussions are to lead toward productivity for the client, the counselor must help the client develop goals and methods of problem solution. The counselor cannot be vague about goal setting, although productive discussions toward these goals must often wait for the client's growth in problem-solving abilities.

Time Frames

The counselor should keep in mind the amount of time needed for each section of the interview. Ideally, all sections of an interview—beginning, discussion, and closing summary—should be completed within the stated time. This is often impossible. Sometimes the verbalization of a problem will encompass the total time allotted. Sometimes clients have urgent problems that must be resolved immediately. Each interview will develop its own time frame based upon needs and changing conditions. As the discussion proceeds, the counselor's ability to balance emphasis on areas of importance becomes a juggling act. The counselor's ability to understand issues clearly and to make wise decisions on the spur of the moment is critical.

Questions the counselor may keep in mind during the discussion include: Is it more important to verbalize basic problems than to solve an urgent short-term problem? Will the client return for further counseling, or is this the only visit? What is the most vital need at the moment? How quickly should the interview be paced? Are the vital issues receiving enough attention?

Interviewing Techniques

Interviewing techniques that will aid a client's growth toward problem solution should be based upon the counselor's esteem for the client. This is shown by the counselor's courtesy, good manners, and friendly attitude. There must be sympathetic understanding of problems, as well as hope for future solutions, as shown by statements such as "You are beginning to cope very well . . . I know how you must feel." Interviewing techniques should show that the counselor's intent is toward the ability of the client to reach personal conclusions. The counselor is ready to present viable alternatives to problem solutions when needed, but at no time will the counselor impose personal mindsets and life-style beliefs upon the client.

Probing

Probing techniques that facilitate the usage of questions and the movement of discussion in an interview are those that assert understanding and interest by saying "uh-huh," "I see," and "Yes, that's interesting." Repeat questions, repeat replies, and ask for further clarification. Use neutral comments and questions such as, "What do you mean?" "Could you tell me more?" "Will you tell me what you have in mind?" "Why do you think this is so?" "Could you tell me why you feel that way?" "Do you have any other reasons for feeling as you do?" "Anything else?"[3]

Listening

The counselor must learn to listen to responses, to keep silent when necessary, to avoid bias by responding to answers neutrally, and to avoid making some answers seem more acceptable than others. When using questions, the counselor must give the client time to think through replies and must listen carefully to whatever is said.

Utilizing Responses

A client's responses to questioning are affected by many factors such as feelings of self worth, ability to confront a problem, and belief in the personal value of counseling. Responses may take many forms, and the counselor must be sensitive to those responses that may show that the client's ego or self-confidence is threatened by the questioning. Some clues are evasion of a direct answer, denial of the problem, depersonalization of the problem, minimizing the problem, and defending oneself to the counselor. The client may seem to be lying or evasive, but may or may not be aware of what is happening. The counselor must be understanding and helpful. He or she must try in every way to ameliorate fears and to help the client solve problems.

Self-confrontation may be a long-term process, and initial self-confrontation sessions may be slow even in settings where the client's ego and self-confidence are bolstered by a thoughtful counselor. Care should be taken to understand a client's reactions when the line of conversation touches areas of etiquette that are outside the counselor's knowledge, especially in areas of ethnic and cultural mores. As counselors work with clients from various backgrounds, knowledge of ethnic and cultural mores should develop.

Sometimes clients forget answers or facts, or they may have problems remembering time sequences and names. Counselor sensitivity and understanding are most necessary at these times. Be aware if an impasse has been reached. An impasse may be caused by a client-counselor personality clash. It may also be attributed to the client's inability to make a choice or to face reality. The counselor, in many problem areas, is a vehicle along the way to problem solution. She or he must be objective in realizing that the true role of a counselor is to forget about self and to think about what is best for the client.

Nonverbal Techniques

For the client who is uncomfortable with verbal communication, a number of techniques may be used. An office equipped with art, candy, and magazines, invites the client to explore visually and by tactile means. Some clients will begin to communicate if they have something to hold or touch while talking. If a client shows an interest in a picture or object, the counselor's comment about the object may open the conversation. Sometimes a game, such as checkers, will invite a client to play and verbalize.

For nonverbalizing clients who have not responded after several sessions, self-awareness techniques may be used with caution. In the behavioral exaggeration technique,[4] the client is asked to become aware of what certain body parts are doing, exaggerate these movements, and then share any thoughts engendered while making these movements.

The counselor guides the client by asking such questions as, "Whom are you hitting? or touching?" These questions, whether answered or not, may help the client become aware of personal feelings. Thomas Skoholt[5] suggests a fantasy technique for use in career counseling in which the counselor tells the client to close his/her eyes and imagine a setting in which the client might like to work. The client responds to questions such as "What do you do there each day of the week? How do you get there?" This fantasy technique is an attempt to visualize and verbalize a future work setting and note the possible implications of this setting on the client's life style. These uses of nonverbal techniques may lead clients to an understanding of problems through verbalization related to bodily actions or fantasy.

Closing the Interview

Knowing when to close an interview is based upon the length of time allotted to the interview as well as psychological and administrative factors. Ideally, an interview should be closed when the problem is solved. But problems in human endeavors do not fit into arranged patterns. In many settings, the interview closes at a certain time because that is the administratively allotted time for closing. Sometimes the interview closes because the client is psychologically unable to profit from further discussion. If the interview has been preplanned and the discussion has progressed well, the counselor will move toward closure when the main goals and purposes are achieved. The counselor and client should agree about the main points of accomplishment and the next steps in problem solution. The client should leave the interview with a feeling of worthwhile goal achievement and a knowledge of the next steps in problem solution.

Summarizing the Interview

An objective account of the interview is needed for future reference, for legal reasons, for inclusion in a case study, and as a summation of what occurred during the interview. Notes may be made during the interview if the note-taking is done efficiently and the client knows what is being written. If notes are not made, the counselor must remember everything of importance that occurs during the interview and record these after the interview. At times, with the client's consent, a tape recorder or a stenographer proficient in shorthand may record the interview.

The summary of an interview may be divided into sections:

1. setting
2. purpose
3. problems to be solved
4. discussion
5. conclusion and referral
6. follow-up

The setting, purpose, conclusion, and referral should be approved and verified by the client. The purpose for the interview should be stated clearly and precisely. The setting may state date, place, name of client, and anything in the setting that aided or detracted the client in problem solving. The discussion section will highlight, objectively, the salient points of the interview. The most important facts should be stated first and those of lesser importance written in descending order of importance. The conclusion and follow-up section will list, in descending order of importance, the items agreed upon by the counselor and client. Included may be steps in problem solution, future plans, and referrals to other agencies. An example of a summary follows.

Example of an Interview Summary

---

1. *Setting*
   Mrs. Williams, forty-five, divorced, is living on welfare but wants to be self-supporting. She is unable to work at many jobs because she has asthma and is allergic to many things. She has just completed her high school diploma through night school.

2. *Purpose*
   Mrs. Williams wants to know how she can gain more education in order to earn a living.

3. *Problems to be solved*
   How can Mrs. Williams get more education in a field where her allergies won't be a problem? How will her education be funded? Which field should she enter?

4. *Discussion*
   Major facts discussed (listed in descending order of importance)
   a. Mrs. Williams prefers to go into business or office work.
   b. The local community college has a business administration program.
   c. She can get to the college by walking five blocks and taking two buses.
   d. County welfare will pay for her tuition and books. She is able to pay bus fare.
   e. She believes she can attend college during the winter when her allergies are not so pronounced. She will not attend summer sessions because she is always ill in the summer.

5. *Conclusions and referral*
   a. Mrs. Williams will attend the fall session of the community college and enroll in the business administration program.
   b. She will make an appointment this week to see a community college counselor to set up her class schedule.
   c. She will find out the bus schedules that meet her class schedules.
   d. She will make application this week for welfare payments for tuition and books.
6. *Follow-up*
   a. Mrs. Williams is scheduled for one more visit in the event she requires additional help.
   b. The counselor will phone Mrs. Williams after the second, fourth, and eighth weeks of college to find out how she is progressing.

Practical Applications of Interviewing Techniques

In order to become effective in the use of interviewing techniques, one must have practice in varying settings. Role playing is an excellent means of simulating interview sessions. This section presents the basis of interviews that may be used for role playing by a counselor and client. To prepare for this role playing, read the section in this book about role playing. With a partner, role play the interviews that are in your counseling field. To evaluate your performances, use the evaluation form provided in this chapter. These may be completed by observers, as well as your partner in role playing. Results should be discussed by all the players involved. Do not be discouraged if your initial role as an interviewer is difficult. Interviewing skills are learned slowly through exposure to many situations.

Problems for Role Playing
Elementary School: Interview 1
COUNSELOR: John has been sent to you because of his negative attitudes toward school. You have been asked to find out how to get John to cooperate.
JOHN: You are nine years of age and do not like your teacher or school. You would rather be with your father fixing cars. Your father believes that schooling is a waste of time for a boy. He makes good money fixing cars and he never went to school. You have been sent to see the counselor because you have not cooperated in reading class during the past few days.

Elementary School: Interview 2

COUNSELOR: Harry, age eleven, has been sent to you to find out why he has been fighting on the school grounds.

HARRY: You are eleven years old. While playing, you fell on a stick and lost the sight of one eye. You now have a glass eye, and the kids call you "Old One Eye." This hurts you very much, and you hate the fact that in many of the school's ball games you cannot see accurately enough to play well.

Secondary School: Interview 1

COUNSELOR: Mary, fourteen, has been away from your suburban school for a month because a carload of men jumped her when she was walking to school and raped her. She was so badly injured she will never be able to have children. She has had counseling at the hospital, and you are to continue with her at school.

MARY: Because of what happened, you are still very nervous and frightened. You like the counselor and want to talk to her about getting back to school routines.

Secondary School: Interview 2

COUNSELOR: Sally's mother phoned and asked you to talk to Sally and persuade her that she should go to college.

SALLY: You want to study hairdressing, but your parents want you to go to college. You are a C student in most subjects and do not want to go to college. All your cousins and friends intend to go to college, and you know your parents have their hopes set on your going as well.

Higher Education: Interview 1

COUNSELOR: Jane has made an appointment to see you about entering college.

JANE: You are forty-five years old and have just completed a divorce settlement in which you are to receive two years of college. This must be completed within thirty-six months. You completed one year of college when you were eighteen, in elementary education. You have no idea what you want to do, but know you must be able to earn a living as soon as possible.

Higher Education: Interview 2

COUNSELOR: Andrew has just dropped into the counseling center and he wants to talk to you because he is very worried.

ANDREW: You are a college senior and cannot concentrate on your studies because your father, who lives nine hundred miles away, is dying of cancer. He wants you to stay in school so that he can experience the pleasure of your graduation. However, you are unable to study because you believe you should be living at home and getting a job. Your family is in dire financial straits because of your father's illness.

Career Counseling: Interview 1
COUNSELOR: You have been asked by the boss of an electrical company to counsel one of his employees who is always late for work and is frequently absent.
PAT: You are twenty-six and a trained electrician. However, you get fired from jobs constantly because you are always late, talk too much, and become very angry when reprimanded. Your present employer, who likes your work, has sent you to the career center to see if you can get yourself straightened around.

Career Counseling: Interview 2
COUNSELOR: Joanne has signed up for an interview but you know nothing about her.
JOANNE: You are thirty-three years old and have taught school for twelve years. The past year you have suffered from "teacher burnout." You are a nervous wreck and have made up your mind that after this year you will never go back to teaching again. You have no idea how you will live and no ideas about possible jobs. You just know you have to get out of the classroom.

Emotional, Drug, and Criminal Problems: Interview 1
COUNSELOR: You are a penal institution's counselor and Pete, who has been attending some religious meetings, has asked to talk to you.
PETE: You have spent fifteen years in and out of jail. Two years ago, a religious group came to the prison. You took their series of lessons in living and are a changed person. Because of the changes you are eligible for parole. The religious group says they will help you enter one of their colleges to prepare for a career. It seems like a good idea, but you are not sure if you should do it.

Emotional, Drug, and Criminal Problems: Interview 2
COUNSELOR: You are a counselor in an alcohol rehabilitation center.
TOM: age twenty-one. You are a truck driver and you realize you are

an alcoholic. You have been sent to the counseling center as part of a court order because you were arrested for driving while drunk. You would like to stop drinking, but you do not know how.

Family Counseling: Interview 1

COUNSELOR: You are a counselor in a center for refugees. You speak several languages.

MINA: You are fifty-eight years old and an Asian refugee who has been in the States for two years. You have a son and a daughter who came with you. Your daughter, who received a music scholarship, has one more year of college left before she obtains her degree. Your son has a job as a lab technician. He has just announced that he can no longer care for you or keep you in his apartment because his girl friend is arriving in five days. They will marry and do not want you or his sister around. You do not speak English and have no job skills. Your daughter says she will quit college and get a job, but you do not want her to lose her educational chances.

Family Counseling: Interview 2

COUNSELOR: Val has told you that his wife is threatening to leave him. You do not know the circumstances.

VAL: You and your wife have a child of five who has only stumps for arms and legs. Your wife has been taking care of the child at home, but the effort has become too great for her now that the child is growing bigger. You do not know how she can continue to cope. She has threatened to leave you, and you know something must be done in the near future.

The Elderly: Interview 1

COUNSELOR: You are the counselor in a pleasant retirement community and know the residents well. Phillip is an active, dissatisfied member of the community.

PHILLIP: You are seventy-eight and in good health. You and your wife have been living in a retirement community for two years. You hate it; your wife loves it. You have an opportunity to go back home and work fifteen hours per week for your old firm. You want to go, but you don't want to upset your wife.

The Elderly: Interview 2

COUNSELOR: You are a counselor who visits people who are home bound. The visiting nurse has suggested that you visit Paul.

PAUL:You are seventy-nine and have heart pains, asthma, head-aches, and sore legs that make walking difficult. You overheard your wife tell a neighbor that you have about a year to live. You are frightened and wish you had a reasonable view of death, but you have no idea what it is. You cannot sleep at night because you are worrying about death.

Observer's Checksheet for Evaluating the Interview (To be used with role playing)

Counselor's Name _____ Date _____	Yes	No	Adequate	Not Adequate	Not Applicable
1. Physical setting is conducive to communication					
2. Preparation for interview					
a. Format of interview is prepared					
b. Key questions are prepared					
c. Background information is available					
3. Counselor					
a. is positive in attitude					
b. is courteous					
c. shows empathy with client					
d. is professional in appearance and manner					
e. records notes efficiently					
4. Beginning Interview Counselor					
a. places client at ease					
b. obtains client's approval for purposes of interview					
5. Discussion					
a. Major problems are discussed					
b. Minor problems are discussed					
c. Discussion is directive					
d. Discussion is non-directive					
6. Interviewing Techniques Counselor					
a. states questions clearly					
b. utilizes responses					
c. listens to responses					

Observer's Checksheet for Evaluating the Interview (To be used with role playing)

Counselor's Name ____ Date ____	Yes	No	Adequate	Not Adequate	Not Applicable
d. uses probing techniques that facilitate discussion					
e. is aware of nonverbalized communication					
7. Closing Counselor					
a. closes interview at an appropriate time					
b. summarizes achievements					
c. provides for follow-up					
d. sends client away with a sense of accomplishment					
8. Total assessment for this interview					

Notes

1. Marjory Brown-Azarowicz, *Individual and Group Assessment Procedures in Reading for Grades 4-7* (Washington, D.C.: University Press of America, 1982), 13.

2. Ibid.

3. Ibid., 16.

4. Zander Ponzo, "Integrating Techniques from Five Counseling Theories," *Personnel and Guidance Journal* 54:8 (April 1976), 417.

5. Thomas Skoholt, "Guided Fantasy In Career Counseling," *Personnel and Guidance Journal* 52:10 (June 1974), 694.

Bibliography

Brown-Azarowicz, Marjory. *Individual and Group Assessment Procedures in Reading for Grades 4-7.* Washington, D.C.: University Press of America, 1982.

Ponzo, Zander. "Integrating Techniques from Five Counseling Theories." *Personnel and Guidance Journal,* 54, no. 8 (April 1976).

Skoholt, Thomas. "Guided Fantasy in Career Counseling." *Personnel and Guidance Journal,* 52, no. 10 (June 1974).

CHAPTER THREE

The Case Study and the Case Conference

The Case Study

The case study is a long-term investigation of a client's problems in which, ideally, professionals of several disciplines pool knowledge, facts, and expertise in order to develop an adequate basis for problem solution. The case study is time-consuming and costly, and is usually reserved for complex cases in which a client may be studied over a period of time. The case study involves all aspects of working with clients including defining the problem, analyzing the data, counseling the client, and developing problem solutions. This chapter is an overview of the basic principles of the case study and the case conference. Details are developed throughout this book.

Steps in a Case Study

The steps in conducting a case study are similar to those for an interview. However, the case study is a more involved process and each aspect is developed in more detail than in the interview. The steps in a case study may be diagrammatically represented.

Steps in a Case Study

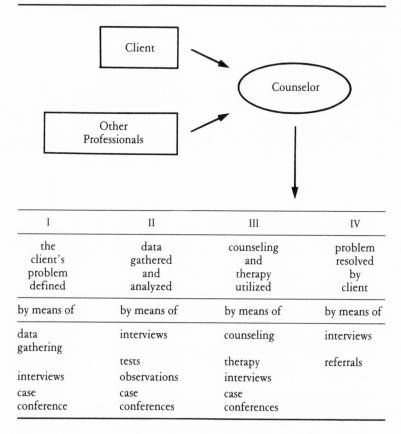

I	II	III	IV
the client's problem defined	data gathered and analyzed	counseling and therapy utilized	problem resolved by client
by means of	by means of	by means of	by means of
data gathering	interviews	counseling	interviews
	tests	therapy	referrals
interviews	observations	interviews	
case conference	case conferences	case conferences	

The client, counselor, and other professionals react with each other and also with each step in the process. The client's problem is defined from available data and by means of interviews and case conferences. Data are gathered from many sources by means of tests, case conferences, observations, interviews, and the like. These data are analyzed by the counselor in collaboration with other professionals and the client. Methods of counseling and/or therapy are developed that are likely to aid problem solution, and many ways of implementation are devised. Finally, the client learns to solve problems and live successfully within the chosen life-style environment. This success may be due to continuing support systems obtained from the counseling or a referral agency. Ideally, a case study would cover all four areas, but due to the variety of problems and problem solutions not all areas are utilized in each study.

Important Elements in a Case Study

The most important elements in a case study are listed below as questions.

1. Which client's problems shall be chosen for a case study from the clients serviced by an agency? Because a case study is time consuming and costly, only a few cases may be studied in depth. Each organization or agency develops its own criteria based upon client needs and the resources of the agency or institution.
2. Which counseling and/or therapy models should be chosen to help a client toward problem solution? From the variety of counseling models in current use, one or more may be of particular value for a particular case. The following table suggests models and possible uses:

Counseling Model	Age Group	Type of Counseling
Behavioral Counseling	Adults Children Teens	Assertiveness training Anxiety lessening Behavior modification in schools, hospitals, institutions
Play Therapy	Children up to eight or nine years	Self-identity Problems with adults and peers Nonverbal Need for emotional growth through play
Person-centered Counseling	Teens Adults with verbal skills	Development of self-concept Need for a non-threatening atmosphere where client may explore capabilities
Existential Counseling	Adults	Helps clients to have inner freedom Problems with death Need to find meaning for life Need to experience life as reality
Reality Counseling	Adults Teens	Behavioral and emotional problems in schools and institutions
Transactional Analysis	Children Adults Groups	Analyses of personal behavior Interpersonal communication People who manipulate others rather than communicating Persons not OK with themselves and others

3. Which professional will be responsible for the case study? One professional is usually responsible for the development of the study. This person should have the knowledge necessary to deal with the problem as well as the ability to have rapport with the client.

4. Which other professionals should be involved? Other professionals are needed in areas where the counselor in charge of the case lacks expertise with a particular problem. The usage of several professionals causes costs to rise. Usage is dependent upon need and availability and whether the professionals work within the agency or outside. If outside, referrals must be made with the client's consent.

5. Which data will be gathered? Sometimes extensive data will be needed; at other times a series of tests will be necessary in order to solve the problem.

6. Which other persons from the client's environment should be brought into the process? With minors and clients who are incapable of decision making or problem solving, parents, guardians, relatives, and friends give major input to problem solutions.

7. Who will analyze the data and the facts in the case? The counselor responsible for the case should have prime responsibility, but in areas where the counselor's knowledge is lacking, other professionals should be brought in. The case conference is a good place for the counselor to seek information and clarification of issues.

8. Is a total solution possible, or should the case aim toward partial solution?

Because of the complexity of human problems, a total solution is not likely. The counselor should keep a goal in mind that is possible to attain within the allotted time frame. A priority of needs may be established and critical problems resolved first.

The Case Conference

The case conference is a meeting of the professionals involved in a case study in order to further problem solution. It may be called for a variety of reasons: to initiate or end the study, to update those involved, to seek knowledge from the group, to obtain ideas in case of an impasse, to obtain help with an analysis of data, and to make recommendations to the client. At times, the client and/or the client's family may come to the case conference.

The values of the case conference are based upon the assumption that a number of professionals collaborating on a client's problems will produce more reliable results than a single counselor. Some of the values are that (1) the pooling of ideas presents a wider range of options for the client, (2) the knowledge of members or of one member may solve a problem, (3) the group may be more objective because it is more removed from the case than the counselor, and (4) the group may have the ability to uncover fallacies in strategy and planning.

The person in charge of a case conference should prepare well for each aspect. The time chosen should be suitable for the participants' schedules. The length of time for the conference should be designated and not overstepped. An agenda and updated reports should be given to all participants before the conference. If the materials are confidential, they should be given out at the beginning of the conference and collected at the end. Participants who have information to present should be given lead time for preparation.

The conference should begin with a clear statement of the items to be discussed and a short presentation of pertinent facts and progress in the case. Participants who have items to share should do so. The priority of the items to be discussed should be decided before the meeting. Participants should be free to disagree and to change priorities. The person in charge should keep track of the time and should try to keep the discussion focused on the priority items. Objective statements should be encouraged, while stereotyped and pat answers to problems are to be avoided. Participants should be encouraged to express views freely. No one should be pressured into positions favored by administrators or the persons in control of the case. The purpose of a case conference is to search out solutions, not to follow preconceived pathways of thought.

The dynamics of group interaction are in operation during a case conference. Persons assume roles and positions on topics. The leader must be alert to these dynamics and use them to the advantage of the study. Persons who take control and lead the conference to their own desires should be avoided. The techniques of free-form discussion and brain-storming are useful when the generation of ideas is stalemated. Beliefs and ideas of each member should be called for and encouraged. As facts and data are presented, they should be collected and the most pertinent items recorded by the person in charge and/or by a recording secretary. As ideas and recommendations are logically developed toward closure, these should be recorded and reread in order to obtain group approval. By the end of the conference, the major facts and recommendations should be recorded and approved by all participants and suggestions for the next steps made.

A well-planned, carefully developed case conference should cause the case to move forward positively. However, participants should realize that in human relations settings, miracles do not always occur. Participants should be encouraged to take positive views of the process and of the clients and their problems.

Follow-up of clients should be immediate and efficient. Evaluation of follow-up procedures should be conveyed to conference participants as should a summary of conference proceedings. With confidential issues, a written statement may not always be given. A short evaluation of conference procedures by participants may expedite future meetings.

Writing Case Study Reports

Writing a case study report is dependent upon the resources and philosophy of the particular agency involved. The content and style are developed by each agency and are governed by its rules. Basic items that should be included are the problem, data, summaries of results of interviews and case conferences, suggestions for problem solution, and the results of implementation. Statements should be objective, brief, and written with clarity. Subjective statements should not be included unless they are valuable to the solution.

A summary of a case study follows. In this case an elderly woman, Mary White, has been brought to the counseling center because of her son's abusive treatment of her. The summary includes the important items discussed during interviews with the principals in the case, and shows the progressive decisions made toward problem resolution.

Summary of a Case Study

I

Date study began _____ Date study ended _____

Counselor _____ Phone _____

Client _____ Age _____

Home Address _____ Phone _____

Business Address _____ Phone _____

Nearest relative, guardian or friend _____

Address _____ Phone _____

II

Reasons for study:

Neighbor, Mrs. George, brought Mrs. White to agency. She had taken her to Dr. Metcalf's office after finding her bruised. Mrs. White's son, who has been out of work for two years, beats his mother periodically.

Major problems (list in order of importance):

1. How may Mrs. White be protected from her son's beatings?

2. Where may she live?

3. Where may she obtain money, for she is a citizen of another country?

4. What help should be given to John White?

Test results:

A medical exam showed severe bruises and some lacerations, but Mrs. White is in good physical and emotional health for her age, despite the way her son has treated her.

III

Interviews:

Jan. 16

A. Major items discussed

1. Mrs. White can live with Mrs. George for a few days.

2. She refuses to go back to live with her son.

3. Mrs. White feels ill from the last beating and wants to rest.

4. Mrs. White has no money. The money she brought from another country has been used by her son.

B. Recommendations
1. Mrs. White will live with Mrs. George for a few days and rest.
2. She will receive a complete physical.
3. Counselor will try to see if she can be placed on county relief.
4. Counselor will seek a permanent place of residence for Mrs. White.

Jan. 18   Mrs. White and Mrs. George
A. Major items discussed
1. Mrs. White can get temporary county relief and housing in a private home.
2. Mrs. White is glad to be away from her son.
3. Mrs. White would like to go back to her own country.
B. Recommendations
1. Counselor will see that Mrs. White obtains her belongings and is settled in a new home.
2. Counselor will talk to son.
3. Counselor will explore possibility of Mrs. White returning to her homeland.

Jan. 22   Counselor and son and his wife
A. Major items discussed
1. Son and family cannot care for mother.
2. Possibility of criminal charges being laid against son.
3. Son has used all of mother's money and cannot give her any money.
B. Recommendations
1. Son will stay away from mother. His wife will visit her and take her belongings to her.
2. Son's wife will give Mrs. White some money each month from her paycheck.
3. Son will come to agency for counseling once a week.

Jan. 30   Counselor and Mrs. White
A. Major items discussed
1. Funds available in U.S. are meager and Mrs. White's living conditions are poor.
2. Mrs. White has written to friends in her own country to find out particulars about the home for the elderly in her native town.

3. Personnel from the embassy of her country said that Mrs. White is possibly eligible for a pension and transportation home.

4. Mrs. White will not press criminal charges against her son.

B. Recommendations

1. Mrs. White will contact more friends in her own country.

2. Counselor will explore options with the embassy.

Feb. 15   Mrs. White, counselor, embassy member

A. Major items discussed

1. Mrs. White has received a letter from the home for the elderly in her own country stating they will accept her March 15.

2. The embassy has found funds for half the transportation cost.

B. Recommendations

1. Mrs. White will write to the home for elderly accepting for March 15.

2. Counselor will search for local funds to pay the rest of the transportation.

Mar. 10   Mrs. White and counselor

A. Major items discussed

1. Counselor has found a private source of funding.

2. Mrs. White understands all arrangements for flight and arrival in her own country.

B. Recommendations

1. Embassy will arrange for transportation to airport, and personnel from the home for the elderly will meet her in her own country.

Mar. 20   Counselor and son

A. Major items discussed

1. Careers and how to get a job.

2. What the agency can do to help him with personal problems.

B. Recommendations

1. Son is to receive career and job counseling.

2. Son is to receive personal counseling over a period of time for his problems.

IV
Conclusion:
Apr.4

1. Mrs. White is settled in her own country and writes that she is happy to be there. She receives board and room and a small pension paid by the government.

2. Her son is receiving career and personal counseling.

3. Her son's wife is sending her a small amount of money each month.

CHAPTER FOUR

Selection of Appropriate Data

In order to facilitate the beginning steps in a case study, data about the problem must be gathered. The counselor needs to make wise judgments based upon knowledge, experience, and common sense. The counselor has a wide fund of testing devices and sources of information that can be used as the basis for the initial steps in problem solution. As the study develops, more data will be gathered to meet developing needs. At each step in the process, the counselor ascertains which data will best serve the purposes of problem solution.

Guidelines for Data Selection

Below are some guidelines that will help the counselor choose data wisely.

1. The problem should be defined clearly. When problems are complex, the various components of the problem may be stated and then data for the solution of each individual component may be chosen.
2. Only data appropriate and relevant to the problem should be considered. For example, if a woman wishes career counseling from an agency, all the data on file about her divorce are irrelevant to her present problem. Only data about her employment, education, and aspirations are relevant.

3. The culture in which the client grew up and in which the client is now living should be examined. This includes the mores and the economic and environmental forces that have affected the client.
4. Longitudinal data are often important. These may show consistency of behavior over a period of time, as well as the relationship between past and present behavior.
5. Emphasis should be upon the significance of the data rather than upon the frequency of occurrence.
6. Data should be gathered until sufficient information is available to help the client make inferences and conclusions that lead to problem solutions.
7. Data should be accurate. At times, however, accurate data may be too expensive or too time-consuming to obtain. The client will need to be aided toward problem solutions without these data.
8. As more data are gathered and the study moves in changing directions, the types of data collected will change. Data gathering and problem solving are fluid, ever-changing processes that are affected by the changing dynamics of the client's life.
9. Data that affect the client's present behavior are more valuable than data about past behavior.

Data Collection Checklist

The following listing of data has been prepared to help counselors decide which types of data may be of most value in a particular case.

Data Collection Checklist

---

1. Personal
   a. Name _____ Birthdate _____
   b. Address _____
   c. Place of birth _____ Home phone _____
   d. Single ___ Married ___ Divorced ___ Widowed ___
                                          Business phone _____

2. Relatives and friends
   a. Spouse _____ Profession _____ Employer _____ Phone _____
   b. Parents _____ Address _____ Phone _____
   c. Stepparents _____ Address _____ Phone _____
   d. Guardian _____ Address _____ Phone _____
   e. Friends _____ Address _____ Phone _____

3. Children
   Name, address, phone, date of birth

4. Other Relatives
   Name, address, phone, date of birth

5. Places of Residence dates (list most recent first)
   Institutions lived in (jails, hospitals)
   Dates (list most recent first)

6. Hobbies

7. Organizations of which a member

8. Physical Health
   a. Height, weight, blood pressure
   b. Heart, lungs, kidneys
   c. Allergies, diabetes, smoking habits
   d. Drinking habits, drug history
   e. History of illness—dates
   f. Communicable diseases—dates
   g. Accidents—dates
   h. Health insurance policies
   i. Cause of parents' deaths
   j. Cause of siblings' deaths

9. Educational History
   a. Elementary schools attended—dates, grades
   b. Secondary schools attended—dates, grades
   c. Trade and community colleges—dates, grades
   d. Colleges attended—dates, grades
   e. Graduate schools attended—dates, grades
   f. Membership in professional organizations
   g. Creative productions
   h. Fields of academic pursuit
   i. Fields of professional pursuit

10. Social Development
    a. Personality tests
    b. Interest inventories
11. Standardized Test Data
    a. IQ tests
    b. Achievement tests
12. Nonstandardized Tests
13. Emotional Development
    a. Tests
    b. Statements from psychiatrists
    c. Statements from mental hospitals
14. Work Experiences (list most recent first)
    a. Employer _____ Salary _____ Dates _____
    b. Fired from _____ Reasons _____ Date _____
    c. Welfare recipient _____ County _____ Dates _____
    d. Retired
    e. Social Security
    f. Supplemental income sources
    g. Attitude toward work
15. Vocational Plans
    a. Tests
    b. Aspirations
    c. Work experiences in high school and college
    d. Internships
16. Referral Agencies
17. Professionals
    a. Medical
    b. Educational
    c. Psychological
18. Other Sources (list)

What Would You Do?

From the following problems, choose those that are in your area of interest. State the data, from the Data Collection Checklist, that you would utilize to aid in problem solution. Which of these are of prime importance? What other types of data are needed?

Elementary and High School Counseling

1. John Govern, age eleven, is in fourth grade. His reading level is 2.1. He has had three years of remedial reading at school and two years in a private clinic. His grades for the past nine weeks were: Reading, D; Arithmetic, C; Social Studies, C; Science, B; P.E., D. The classroom teacher thinks he should be in a special class. His parents do not wish this. Where should he be placed in the school system? What should be done for him?

2. Miss Jones, a fourth grade teacher, is very concerned about Joel Adams, age eight, who comes to school with black-and-blue marks all over his body. Recently he had bleeding welts on his back. Joel insists that he is clumsy and falls a lot. What can be done to find out the causes?

3. Charles Foley, age sixteen, has just been proclaimed state boxing champion for his age level. His grade average is D + and his reading level is grade 5.4. He wants to quit school and devote full time to boxing. He has a part-time coaching job that provides him with a car and enough money for board and room. What is the best approach to his future?

4. Joanne Williams, age sixteen, eleventh grade, unmarried and pregnant, wants to keep her baby. She would like to stay in school until graduation and to prepare for a job at which she could earn a living for herself and her baby. Her last report shows the following grades: English, C; S.S., C; Music, B; P.E., B; Science, C; Math, C. How may the school help her?

College Counseling

1. Mary has been going to college for four semesters and has taken courses in many disciplines. She has not declared a major and

has no idea what she would like to do. In her first year, she registered in elementary education; the second year, in business administration. She did not enjoy either field. She has come to the counseling center to find direction for her life.

2. Jim has completed his first semester in college and has grades of C and D in all his subjects. In high school, he was an A student. This is his first experience away from home, and he has found that dormitory life and studying are difficult. He wants to know how to improve his study habits.

Family Counseling

1. Jane has some broken ribs and broken fingers after being beaten by her husband. She is afraid to go back to him but believes a woman is nothing without a husband. She has no place to live and doesn't know what to do with her life. She has come to the counseling center from the hospital and needs immediate help.

2. Mary, age seventeen, is afraid to go home because her mother's new husband has made advances toward her. She is unable to explain the problem to her mother, and would like to move out of the house and live on her own.

Career Counseling

1. Mr. Ellsworth, age forty-two, has just retired from the air force and would like a job in civilian life. He has a master's degree in government and two years of a business administration degree. Where can he find work?

2. Mrs. Jessup, age thirty-eight, divorced, has a teaching degree in elementary education. She does not want to teach school and be involved in modern-day discipline problems. She would like to prepare for a job outside of academia. How may she find out which professions would be best for her?

Counseling Those with Emotional and Criminal Problems

1. John Jamieson, age twenty-one, is in jail for theft. He is an inner-city male with nine years of schooling. John likes to work with sports cars and would like to be a mechanic of German

sports cars. In grade nine, his grades were: English, B; Math, C; Reading, grade 4.5; Typing, C; Shop, B. What can be done for him in a jail setting?

2. Mrs. Barnes, age thirty-five, separated, has two children, ages six and nine, who live with her in an apartment paid for by her step-mother. Her husband sends her some money for food. Clothing is given to her by a church group. Mrs. Barnes has been in and out of mental hospitals since early childhood and has difficulty ordering her life, keeping house, and looking after her children. Her husband phones her often and tells her how stupid and ugly she is. After these calls, she goes to bed with a headache for two days. What can be done to help this family?

Counseling the Aged

1. Mrs. Jane Otis, age sixty-five, widowed, lives alone on a pension in Los Angeles. Her only daughter lives in Boston and would like her mother to live nearby. Mrs. Otis cannot live with her daughter because her daughter's husband is a person who makes life miserable for everyone. What can be done to bring mother and daughter closer together in living arrangements?

2. Tom Pope, age seventy, has been a widower two years but cannot get over the death of his wife. He spends many hours every day in meditation and goes to a spiritualistic seance each week to hear his wife speak to him from another world. His children are very worried about him. What can be done to help Mr. Pope in his unhappiness?

Answer Checksheet

Elementary and High School Counseling

1. The case of John Govern

   1: a, b, c; 2 b; 6; 8; 9 a; 10: a, b; 11: a, b, 12; 13 a; 15 b; 17: a, c.

   The most important items are (a) a complete physical, (b) psychological assessment, (c) a battery of achievement tests, (d) interest inventories, and (e) his educational history. Medical and psychological professionals may be brought in at a future date. The first question to answer is: "Does John meet the city-state requirements for special services?" Later data gathering will depend upon the parents' reactions to the data gathered.

2. The case of Joel Adams

1: a, b, c; 2 b; 4; 5; 8; 9 a; 16; 17 a.

To be checked out are the possibilities of child abuse, and any health problems that result in bruised skin. Of prime importance is a complete medical assessment followed by facts about previous skin damage from all persons who know Joel. Referral to a county child-abuse center would be a next step if the medical check did not show a skin-related disease.

3. The Case of Charles Foley

1: a, b, c; 2: b, e; 6; 7; 8; 9: a, b, i; 14: a, f, g; 15: a, b, c.

Of prime importance are (a) physical health, (b) ability in and attitude toward a boxing career, (c) the attitudes of his parents, and (d) his ability to hold a job and stay with it.

4. The Case of Joanne Williams

1: a, b, c, d; 2: b, c; 8; 9: a, b, h, i; 10: a, b; 11 b; 15: a, b, c; 16.

She needs to be aware of (a) her interests and abilities and (b) the ways in which she can prepare for the job market. Achievement tests and interest inventories would be important, as well as referral to agencies or institutions where she could obtain knowledge about possible careers.

College Counseling

1. The Case of Mary

1: a, b; 9: a, b, c, d, g, h; 10: a, b; 11: a, b; 12; 13 a; 14: a, b, g; 15: a, b, c.

The most important items are (a) Mary's emotional health, (b) her attitudes toward the world of work, and (c) achievement test results. Interest inventories and referrals to career counseling may help her make decisions. Data about her work experiences may lead to problem solutions.

2. The Case of Jim:

1: a, b; 11: a, b; 12; 14: a, g; 15: a, b.

Jim's basic academic abilities should be checked for strengths and weaknesses. Nonstandardized tests that probe study skills are of prime importance, as are his experiences and attitudes toward work and his knowledge of the possibilities of matching his abilities with the professions and the world of work.

Family Counseling

1. The Case of Jane

   1: a, b; 2: a, b, e; 3; 4; 6; 7; 8; 9: a, b, d, h, i; 10; 14: a, g; 15: a, b; 16.

   Because Jane needs help immediately, she should be referred to an agency that can care for her physical needs until she can support herself. Friends and relatives who might help her should be known. Batteries of achievement, interest, and aptitude tests would give insights into her potential abilities, as would her attitudes toward the world of work. Of immediate importance is her physical health. Data on attitudes toward herself as a woman and her goals in life would help to place her problems in focus.

2. The Case of Mary

   1: a, b; 2: b, e; 4; 16; 17: b, c.

   Mary needs a place to live immediately. Friends, relatives, or agencies that could provide for her should be noted. After her immediate needs are met, her mother, as well as support persons in her life, should be contacted. Her problem may be helped through psychological counseling.

Career Counseling

1. The Case of Mr. Ellsworth

   1: a, b, c, d; 6; 7; 8; 9: c, d, e, f, g, h, i; 14; 15: a, b, f, d; 16.

   Mr. Ellsworth needs to have his abilities related to the current job market. His skills, college degrees, and work experiences should be known, as well as the job market in the areas of the country where he would be willing to work. Up-to-date job market analyses should be available.

2. The Case of Mrs. Jessup

   1: a, b; 6; 7; 8; 9 d, e, f, g, h, i; 10: b; 11: a, b; 14: a, f, g; 15: a, b, c.

   Stating what she is able to do with present skills is of importance. Tests to uncover her abilities should include interest inventories and listing of hobbies. Because her work experiences and college preparation are limited to educational pursuits, she needs to survey the needs of the local job market through an agency specializing in this field. She should be guided to match her interests and abilities with an educational program which will prepare her for the job market.

Counseling Those with Emotional and Criminal Problems

1. The Case of John Jamieson

   1: a, b; 6; 9: a, b; 10: a, b; 14: a, b, c, f, g; 15: a, b, c; 16.

   John knows what he wants to do and knows the areas of his greatest interests and ability. Initial data should include the educational services offered in prison, by correspondence, or by attendance at a nearby institution. Data on John's work habits and attitudes would show if he could profit from opportunities for study. Finally, personality, achievement, and interest tests would give John a clearer understanding of his true abilities.

2. The Case of Mrs. Barnes

   1: a, b, d; 2: a, b, c, e; 3; 8; 10 a; 13: a, b, c; 16; 17: a, c.

   The clients are not only Mrs. Barnes but also the children. Thus, of prime importance are data on the physical and emotional health of the children and how they are coping educationally, emotionally, and socially. Which persons give them emotional support? Which agencies could supplement support? The next area of data gathering is to find agencies, relatives, or friends who would ascertain that food, clothing, and shelter were always available even if the mother were in the hospital. Data are needed on referral agencies where Mrs. Barnes and her children could be taught housekeeping and money management skills. Finally, data are needed about agency support systems to help Mrs. Barnes through periods of emotional crisis.

Counseling the Aged

1. The Case of Mrs. Otis

   1: a, b; 3; 6; 7.

   Very little standardized data are needed. Commonsense data would include places of residence near her daughter's home. Her residence must have access to transportation, religious institutions, and places where Mrs. Otis may pursue her hobbies, belong to organizations of interest, and be near medical facilities.

2. The Case of Tom Pope

1: a, b, c, d; 2 e; 3; 4; 5; 6; 7; 10: a, b; 16; 17.

Of prime importance are (a) persons or agencies where Mr. Pope may receive counseling and (b) names of friends and organizations that can help him pursue forgotten interests. Names of professionals who deal with death and dying in positive ways may be useful in counseling Mr. Pope's family, as well as Mr. Pope.

CHAPTER FIVE

Analysis of Data

Four questions involved in the effective analysis of data are discussed in this chapter. These are: What do the terms used in standardized testing really mean? How should standardized and non-standardized tests or inventories be analyzed? How should data be presented to clients? How may clients be led toward problem solution? In order to analyze data effectively, the counselor must have a knowledge of the values and the problems found within each standardized and non-standardized test. This knowledge is the province of other books and is not dealt with in this text.

The Meanings of Terms in Standardized Tests

Some terms that need clarification are: grade placement scores, intelligence quotients, scaled scores, aptitude, percentiles, equivalent scores, comparable scores, norms, personality, and health scores. The following explanations indicate the cautions needed in the usage of these terms in test interpretation.

Grade Placement Scores

Grade placement scores on achievement tests are averages of the test results of thousands of students on the same test according to the particular grade and month in that grade for each student. Scores are divided into ten equal parts for each grade and month; for example, 3.0, 3.1, 3.2, and so on. A student who receives a particular grade-level score is said to be able to perform near that grade level in the skills tested. The grade placement score is an oversimplification of a student's ability. It is a generalized score and does not present specific details of strengths and weaknesses. These may be obtained from criterion-referenced tests that assess ability according to specified criteria and ability levels.

When analyzing grade placement scores, it should be noted that division into ten points for the school year is an artificial placement not related to individual growth. In reality, an individual's growth is in spurts and plateaus, not in equal units of ten per year. The precise number, 3.0 or 3.6, means little except in the context of all known factors about the person's achievement. Because the grade placement score is generalized, the student with a 3.0 and the student with a 3.6 grade placement score may be achieving at the same level. Since the subject matter covered in a school system may differ widely from that tested by the standardized test, the grade placement score may be meaningless.

Another problem is that different schools, school systems and areas of the country have differing levels of achievement. A 3.0 may be an excellent score in one school, while in another school a 3.0 may be a poor score. Thus, the interpretation of grade placement scores to clients should be made in the light of relevant factors.

Care should be taken in the interpretation of very high scores. For example, a third grade student who scores grade 8.0 in a reading achievement test is not necessarily ready to compete with students in an eighth grade classroom. Scores beyond the normal grade range are usually found by the use of the statistical technique called extrapolation, and the score is not a true score. The student also may not have the background of experiences necessary for complete understanding at the eighth grade level. The student is, in effect, an excellent third-grade reader with much better than third-grade abilities. Placement of such a student in classes achieving more than one or two grades above grade level should be made with caution.

Grade placement scores can be very misleading. For example, a third-grade student with a grade placement score of 6.1 for reading and 4.8 in mathematics may not rank higher in reading than in mathematics when compared to other third-grade students. Both scores may be in the 98th percentile for the class. Mathematics achievement, more than reading, is dependent upon what is taught and "is spread over a narrower range at any one grade"[1]

Intelligence Quotients

There are two ways in which the Intelligence Quotient (IQ) is reported, the ratio IQ and the deviation IQ. The ratio IQ represents the ratio between the chronological age (CA) and the mental age (MA). The MA is obtained by testing a person's performance on tasks completed successfully by others at each age level. The ratio IQ is reported as:

$$IQ = \frac{100 \, MA}{CA}$$

The deviation IQ is based upon the Stanford revision of the Binet Simon scale developed by L. M. Terman, in which the mean is 100 and the standard deviation (SD) is 16. This is a standard score and is the most widely used scoring procedure for IQ. Despite much controversy over the value of IQ scores in assessing individuals, counselors will probably be using the results of these tests in the foreseeable future. The IQ is helpful as a general screening device because it will identify the retarded, as well as those with exceptional abilities in solving the problems of the test. A high IQ does not mean that a person is a genius, but it does show that the person is capable of solving the problems of the test which, in most cases, are related to doing well in school. If a person with a high IQ score does not do well in school, it may be due to the nature of the school's program in relation to the individual's learning methods and patterns of problem solving.

Due to test variations, the IQ will vary from test to test. A happy, warm, or nurturing environment may cause an increase. The IQ may decrease because of brain damage, a severe physical illness affecting the functioning of the brain, schooling deprivation, or a poor home environment. The IQ seems to stay constant in most instances, but this is attributed partly to the properties of the mean and standard deviation, as expressed statistically. The IQ is particularly useful in assessing the probable ability of a child to succeed in school.

Much controversy has raged over the unfairness of IQ scores in testing minorities or those from deprived academic and economic backgrounds. The usual IQ test items are unfair to these groups because the items are culturally biased. The minority or deprived person's real ability and survival intelligence are not measured. However, the IQ tests do show how individual children from minority or deprived cultures are likely to survive and compete in middle-class life. Many culture-free tests are on the market, and some will help the counselor estimate true intelligence. However, if the minority person's goal is to compete in the middle-class job market, the culture-free tests are not of much value because they eliminate items that are related to middle-class knowledge and value systems.

The interpretation of IQ scores is: (1) scores above 160 are extremely high in relationship to the scores made by the total population; (2) 130 to 160 are very high scores; (3) 115 to 130 are above-average scores; (4) 90 to 115 are in the range of about 60 percent of the population; (5) 80 to 90 are low-average; (6) 60 to 80 are low; and (7) below 60 is very low.

Comparison of IQs

The deviation IQ of one test cannot be compared with the deviation IQ of another test, unless they both have the same or similar values for the standard deviations (SD). A ratio IQ and a standard deviation IQ are not comparable. Thus, the counselor needs to know the type of IQ score under consideration and the value of the standard deviation (SD).

Scaled Scores

A scaled score is a statistical description of test performance. It notes the deviation of an individual score from the average as found by standardized procedures. The following scores are scaled scores.

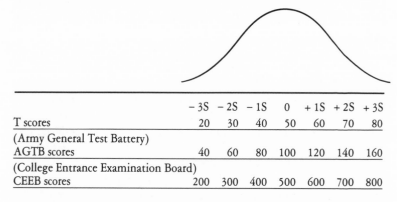

	– 3S	– 2S	– 1S	0	+ 1S	+ 2S	+ 3S
T scores	20	30	40	50	60	70	80
(Army General Test Battery) AGTB scores	40	60	80	100	120	140	160
(College Entrance Examination Board) CEEB scores	200	300	400	500	600	700	800

A particular score should not be considered good or bad. Scores show a deviation from the average. For example, a score of 85 on scale AGTB shows a score below average by less than 1 standard deviation. Scaled scores are useful in equating one test with another on a standard scale. For example, if a client receives 100 on the AGTB and 500 on the

CEEB, the two scores are at the mean of the population. They show the same value according to the population upon whom both tests were standardized. If two tests have been normed according to the same or similar populations and test parameters, comparisons may be made from one test in an academic area to another test in the same area. A scaled score may be used to compare an individual's growth in ability or achievement with past performance, provided the normative data between tests are the same or similar.

Aptitude

An aptitude is a "condition or set of characteristics regarded as symptomatic of an individual's ability to acquire, with training, some knowledge, skill, or set of responses, such as the ability to speak a language, to produce music. . . ."[2] Before one may say that a test predicts, numerous studies should have shown that the test does predict an aptitude for a certain area of learning. The prediction may be only in areas where studies have been done and if the two groups have been normed on similar items.

Percentiles

Percentiles are stated in scores on a scale of 100 points. A percentile score of 78 means that 78 of every 100 individuals who took the test scored less than the individual with the percentile of 78.

> Percentiles probably are the safest and most informative numbers to use provided their two essential characteristics are made clear: (1) that they refer not to percent of questions answered correctly but to percent of people whose performance the student has surpassed, and (2) who, specifically, are the people with whom the student is being compared. The second point—a definite description of the comparison or "norm" group is especially important in making the meaning of test results clear.[3]

The percentile rank is useful only if the group on which it is referenced is known and is comparable. Percentile ranks are not equal units. The counselor should be aware that the difference between a 97 and 98 percentile rank is not the same as between a 57 and 58 percentile rank. Note also that percentile ranks may not be added or averaged.

Achievement scores in percentiles indicate that above 98 is extremely high, above 90 is high, 65-90 is very good, 40-60 is average, 15-40 is weak, and below 15 is very weak.

Equivalent Scores

Test scores are equivalent if they can be substituted for each other. The trait being measured and the means of measurement must correspond between two test scores if they are to be considered equivalent.

Comparable Scores

Two scores may be said to be comparable if they represent the same standing in the same population.

Norms

Norms are the most important factors in analyses. Without equal and comparable norms, nothing can be said about comparisons between test results.

It is important to know the exact population upon which standardized tests were normed. The area of the country, the kinds of persons tested, and the exact location of the testing centers should be stated clearly and specifically. The specifics of the normative population are found in few test manuals. Much caution should be exercised in dealing with the norms stated in test manuals. Norms tend to be generalized and sketchy and rarely meet the standards defined in this paragraph. Thus, all comparisons between standardized tests should be stated with many reservations.

Personality Inventory Scores

Personality inventory scores are usually indicated in standard deviation scores. These show that the normal score is usually between one standard deviation below the mean and one standard deviation above the mean. Counselors should stress the normalcy of the scores where possible. Persons who score two or more standard deviations above or below the mean show traits that are different from those persons upon whom the tests were standardized. However, a score above the second standard deviation above the mean is not ''better'' than a score below the second standard deviation below the mean on a personality inventory. These scores show only that the measured trait is different from the normed scores.

Health Records

Health records are an adjunct to interpretation of a client's background. They should be assessed from the point of view of the present. How does the client's previous health problems affect the present? Extensive historical knowledge of a client's health patterns is not always needed. If a client is presently always on time for work and performs tasks efficiently, the fact that the client was in a hospital for three years is irrelevant to a problem dealing with job placement.

Medical data should be placed in perspective as part of the total picture about the client and should be based upon the interpretation presented by the medical professionals involved.

Analyses of the Results of Standardized Tests

A test measures only those items tested. Even the most widely used tests are not fairy wands or magic potions that present us with answers to life's problems. Each test presents the counselor with a few facts about a client. A number of tests will present a number of facts. These will be relevant to problem solution only if the tests are related to the problem. The facts garnered from standardized tests should be placed in perspective with other facts known about the client's problems and should be weighed according to the value of the particular test toward problem solution. If a client were having academic problems, intelligence and academic achievement scores would be of much more value in problem solution than if the client were having home and family problems. The amount of emphasis placed upon a fact is dependent upon common sense and the counselor's experience with similar cases. As a counselor works with tests, some tests come to the fore as more helpful than others in assessing particular problems. Care must be taken to insure that a counselor does not develop set patterns of values about test results. A flexible and continually open-minded approach to the value of testing instruments needs to be maintained if test results are to be optimally effective in problem solution.

Standardized test results are more readily interpreted if reported in percentiles. If comparisons are to be made between previous and present scores, all items listed under 9 in the Checksheet for Standardized Tests must be positive. Many times, the information needed to answer the questions on the checksheet is unavailable. Test scores are presented, but no publishers' manuals are available. Even when they are available, they do not state clearly the norming population or list comparable tests and scoring procedures. In this dilemma, the scores should be analyzed and interpreted with caution. Every effort must be made to obtain data from publishers, to demand that such materials are made available, and to develop local norms and knowledge about standardized tests to supplement the meager fare offered currently by test publishers.

Individual standardized tests such as the Stanford Binet or the Rorschach are interpreted within the limits of the written statements presented by the psychologist who gave the test.

How does a counselor go about analyzing standardized tests?

1. The client's problems are reviewed and test results are skimmed to note any items that are particularly relevant.
2. The test results are read and checked against relevant criteria. The following checksheet of data items may be used for this purpose.

Checksheet for Analysis of Standardized Tests

	Yes	No	Partially

1. Test is normed upon a population similar to client's
    a. educational background
    b. cultural background			

2. Test is related to or relevant to client's problem			
3. Test is written near client's level of reading ability			
4. Items are written in a style and in language patterns with which client is familiar			
5. Client was motivated to perform well on the test			
6. Client has previously taken a similar type of test			

7. Test results are reported as
    a. grade level scores
    b. percentiles
    c. scaled scores
    d. standard scores
    e. raw scores
    f. other			

8. IQ scores are reported as a
    a. ratio IQ
    b. deviation IQ			

9. Scores that are to be compared
    a. have similar population norms
    b. have same scoring method (e.g. both are percentiles)
    c. can be substituted for each other
    d. measure similar traits, qualities, or knowledge			

3. Notes are made of the most pertinent data from the standardized test scores. These data are those that answer the following questions:
   a. Are the data relevant to the problem?
   b. Do the tests and scores meet most of the requirements for test authenticity and value discussed in this chapter?
   c. Will the test data enhance problem solution?
4. The notes made from the test data are written in descending order of importance to the solution of the problem. For example, Joanne, twelve years of age, cannot read or keep up with her fourth-grade class. In going over the data, it is noted that under "hearing loss" the examiner has said "severe" and "student should be referred to a physician. She may have some type of blockage of both ears." This item would take precedence over "Reading level: grade 2.8." In the data is a statement from Joanne's third grade teacher that should be given priority: "The week of May 4, Joanne seemed changed. She acted like a normal child and learned more words than over the previous six months. She said she was taking antibiotics for an infection." These facts should cause the counselor to question the data stating IQ = 56 and spelling ability = grade 1.8. If Joanne has a severe hearing loss and one teacher has noticed that Joanne learned normally when on antibiotics, a complete diagnosis by an eye-ear-nose-and-throat specialist is the most pertinent next step.

An Example of Data Analysis

Date _____

Name _____ Age ___ Grade ___

Address _____ Referred by _____

Phone _____

Problem: Low reading ability; cannot keep up with classwork

Data (in descending order of importance)
1. Hearing loss: severe—should see physician
2. Grade 3 teacher: May 4. See enclosed statement.
   Joanne's learning ability was much improved when on antibiotics
3. IQ = 56
4. Reading level scores:
   Grade 1 = 1.2
   Grade 3 = 1.8
   Grade 4 = 2.8
5. Joanne was retained in grade 1 and grade 3 for an extra year
6. Personality inventories show anger and frustration. Teacher comments, "Seems angry in reading class. Threw reader against wall and cried."

Analyses of Non-Test Data

Besides standardized tests and health record forms, there are many informal inventories and non-test techniques that may be used to enhance the data gathered about a client's problems. Chapters 7, 8, and 9 discuss the uses of these methods. The knowledge gained from these sources should be incorporated into the data category on the data analysis form. It must be kept in mind that non-test techniques are not standardized. They are more subjective in interpretation than standardized tests. Thus, they are more prone to errors in interpretation than the more objective data of standardized tests. However, non-test techniques may provide insights and understandings of problems and may present a richer background about a client's problems than the results of standardized tests.

For example, Joanne's taped autobiography stated: "My Dad is great. He has taught me how to tune up his car. I can change the spark plugs and the oil. I can hardly wait until I am sixteen and can get my driver's license and am strong enough to change a tire." This presents a picture of Joanne that could not be obtained from standardized tests. These data will be placed high on the data analysis list of "most important facts" discovered about Joanne's problem. From this autobiography, we know that her oral language is grammatically correct and that a major interest is cars. This interest might be developed into a reading interest in stories about cars or learning to read the driver's test manual.

Presentation of Test Data to Clients

The reason for testing is to obtain data that will help the client with problem solutions. However, presentation of the facts about a client's abilities, life history, and problems may be a traumatic experience for the client. It may be misunderstood unless the counselor presents the data wisely and with clarity. Counselors should remember the trauma experienced in college when grades were posted on a bulletin board. To have one's life or one's year-long efforts reduced to a few numerals on a page is a traumatic experience for a person with a strong ego. For an insecure person, it may be devastating. The client must be led to look objectively at data, and at past and present life styles. The client should be helped to develop problem-solving strategies and to plan positively for the future. If the presentation of facts is a traumatic experience, the client may not be able to take steps toward problem solution, and the garnering of data will have been wasted time and effort.

All efforts should be focused upon helping clients know that problem solution is possible. The following guidelines for data presentation should lead toward positive results.

1. Present data positively. Give a client hope about problem solutions. Use positive statements such as, "Your score on this test showed that you have strong abilities in _____." "Your diligence in completing all items, carefully, showed that you have similar abilities to those persons who work in the trade you wish to enter."

2. Present data objectively. Omit your own personal opinions and judgments. State facts and avoid statements such as "In my opinion" or "I believe."

3. Present the most important data first, if possible. Clients will tend to remember first items on a list and will be impressed with them as clues to problem solution. However, if items of prime importance are negative, they should be preceded by positive reinforcement and stated in a nonthreatening manner. "You stated that your prime goal in life was to become an engineer, yet your highest scores are in the humanities and your lowest scores in areas related to engineering."

4. Use layperson's language when describing test results. Omit the jargon of your profession. Draw diagrams and explain results with clarity. Avoid giving exact scores, if possible. A score seems so definitive, unreal, and frightening. An IQ in the 55th percentile might be explained this way: "This test has shown your intelligence to be in the average range. If we took all the people in the world and lined them up according to intelligence, you would be standing on the right side of the halfway mark. This test shows your general intelligence to be average—a little above the middle of the population. You may never be a nuclear physicist or graduate from Harvard with honors, but those are not your goals."

5. After all pertinent data have been presented, ask the client to identify the most important aspects of the data for problem solution. In this way, the client states his/her beliefs and begins to think about problem solutions.

6. As the counseling process proceeds, the client should be encouraged to reach his or her personal solutions to problems. Chapters 10 and 11, Models of Counseling I and II, present the basic models that counselors may use with clients. The goal in most of these models is to help the client find ways in which problems may be solved. For some clients, this step will be spontaneous; for others, it will be difficult. If the client cannot think of any ways to solve the problem, the counselor should present two or three alternative methods. The client must then decide which of these is best.

Jackson stated that "the success of the chosen course of action will depend upon the care and skill put into the part of the plan dealing with implementation."[4] Much effort must be expended in making certain that the client thoroughly understands the problem and is then encouraged to expand upon the acquired data. The counselor must realize that human problems may not be solved readily. Only a part of the solution, or a beginning toward that goal, may be entertained. Sometimes the problem may not be solved. However, the client's attitudes toward a problem may be changed so that the client is able to live positively with the problem.

Helping Clients toward Problem Solution

Ways in which the client may be led toward problem solution include the following.

1. The counselor presents two or three ideas, and the client chooses from these possible methods. Many people can develop ideas from prepared formulas or basic ideas but cannot think up solutions or ideas for themselves. Because the counselor has been involved in defining the problem and gathering data, many ideas will have been generated. The most pragmatic of these may be presented to the client.
2. Problem solutions may evolve from the way in which the data have been presented. In many cases, the solution to the problem is obvious. In the case of Joanne, the first data presented dealt with her deafness. Thus, the initial step in problem solution would be to have a complete assessment by a competent specialist of her deafness.

3. The forced choice technique may be used with clients who seem unable to utilize any of the other problem-solving methods. The counselor presents a series of problem solutions, or steps in solution, with viable alternatives. The client must choose one solution. For example, a prisoner in a penal institution who is studying for his high school diploma has found it difficult to concentrate on his work because of the proximity of a female teacher. The counselor presents him with the following choices: (a) go to class with a guard standing beside him, (b) go to a class with a male teacher, or (c) take the course by correspondence. The client is thus forced to make a decision.

4. Use brainstorming techniques to develop many ideas for problem solution. This technique usually takes time to learn. In brainstorming, ideas are expressed freely. Each individual presents as many thoughts as possible about problem solution within a short period of time. All ideas, whether viable or not, are accepted. Judgments about the values of ideas that are presented are suspended. Brainstorming is premised upon the belief that if a group of people freewheel with a quantity of ideas, at least one worthwhile idea will be generated. The counselor and client may brainstorm together for five or ten minutes. Each person expresses his or her ideas, while remaining receptive to the ideas of the other. They then try to expand upon all the ideas that have been generated.

5. Use charts listing the order in which things must be accomplished. Establish definite dates by which these items must be completed. For example, if a woman wished to change careers, she might set up the following time frame:

   a. Find out from my personnel office what must be done to obtain a leave of absence by March 1.
   b. Find a real-estate agent who would suggest how much my house will rent for if I decide to go back to school by March 5.
   c. Take a battery of aptitude and interest tests by March 15.
   d. Visit the university I would like to attend and find out costs and options by March 25.
   e. Explore the part-time job market by March 30.
   f. Talk to my married son and daughter to let them get used to the idea by April 1.
   g. Explore loans and available scholarships by April 15.

6. Choose parts of a problem to solve. In many instances, the client's total problem is too difficult or involved to solve quickly or completely, but parts of the problem may be solved. Choosing the part to solve is a first approach with many clients. For example, May, age thirty-eight, lives with her active eighty-five-year-old mother who criticizes her constantly. May has come to a point in her life where she cannot take any more of the criticism. However, she does not wish to abandon her mother. With the counselor's help, she decides to solve part of her problem. She rents an apartment in the neighborhood and hires a lady to help her mother with the heavy housework and to make her evening meal. Thus, May has lessened the time spent with her mother, but she still lives near enough to be there when needed. She has solved part of a problem, and is able to live successfully with the rest of the problem.

7. Use decision-making diagrams to help clients plan problem solutions. These diagrams might be called decision trees. They may be of any size or shape, and evolve as the client develops problem-solving skills. Their usefulness lies in their implicit clarity and simplicity. The problem is stated on the first stem of the tree and the possible solutions are developed on the branches. For example, John, age nineteen, whose mother committed suicide, feels very depressed and cannot make himself go to classes. He takes drugs to make himself feel better. His father has remarried and John feels that he is not wanted at home by his stepmother or his brothers and sisters. He would like to have some direction in life and a reason for living. He was never very close to his mother and feels guilty that he was often mean to her. The decision tree clarifies the alternatives as John sees them. Then he can choose which part of the decision tree he wishes to follow. When a choice is made, the positive and negative aspects of this decision are developed. John's decision trees might be developed as follows:

Step 1: A decision tree of present needs

Leave home

Live with father

Leave college

Which direction?

Go into therapy for depression

Go to church

Live in a drug rehabilitation center

Family counseling

Stay in college

Step 2: Second steps in decision-making

Leave home

Live in a drug rehabilitation center

Leave college

Go into therapy for depression

Step 3: A decision tree for the future

Live in a drug rehabilitation center

Return to college

Get a job

Make new friends

Continue therapy for depression

Tree branches that have been completely rejected are to get a job, go to church, family counseling, and to live with his father.

8. When the counselor is unable to help a client toward problem solution, the client should be referred to some other agency or professional.

Within each community there are professionals and agencies that will supplement and extend the value of counseling. Because each counselor's abilities and training have limits, the help of other professionals is sometimes needed. Counselors should be prepared to refer clients to the most competent professional services available. Each counselor should develop a network of contacts, an up-to-date filing system, and established procedures for information transfer between agencies and professionals. Community contacts may be made through professional meetings, searches of local resources, visits to business and industrial concerns, and educational institutions. Information that will be disseminated to clients should specify the exact services offered, the costs involved, and current appraisals of quality.

Many communities have well-established systems that disseminate information through the local media and newsletters distributed to libraries, schools, churches, and synagogues. From these master listings, each counselor must develop a file that has been researched personally. The counselor must know the strengths and weaknesses of each agency or professional to whom referrals are made. A poor referral may negate the value of the counselor's efforts, whereas a good referral will enhance counseling. Provision must be made for clients who wish to choose their own referrals, or who wish to receive second opinions about the counseling they have received.

Problem Examples for Analysis

Example 1

Colleen, eight, in third grade, has been having difficulty in reading. The following *standardized test scores* are available:

- Grade 1, Peabody Picture Vocabulary, IQ 118[5]
- Grade 3, Otis-Lennon, IQ 105
- Kindergarten Readiness from the Gates McGinitie Reading Tests[6]

Subtest	Raw Score	Stanine	Weight	Weighted Score
1. Listening Comprehension	12	4	1	4
2. Auditory Discrimination	11	2	2	4
3. Visual Discrimination	20	6	2	12
4. Following Directions	9	4	2	8
5. Letter Recognition	12	5	3	15
6. Visual-Motor Coordination	12	5	1	5
7. Auditory Blending	7	4	1	4
8. Word Recognition	8	4	Total Weighted Score	52

Readiness Standard Score = 44   Readiness Percentile Score = 27

Informal inventories yield the following data:
1. *Biography.* In a taped (oral) biography, Colleen stated "My brother and sisters and I go to the library every week. My mother lets me take out four books each week. My big sister Norah reads these to me. Sometimes I read a book to myself, but I always feel tired when I read."
2. *Books I Have Read.* Colleen told the teacher she had read two Dr. Seuss books and one book about dinosaurs. She said she would like to read the same books as her sister Norah can read.
3. *Report Card Reading Grades.*

> First Grade: B
> Second Grade: C
> Third Grade (Third month): D

What do these scores mean? What additional information would you need in order to explain the meanings of these scores?

Example 2

Andrew is in eighth grade and is very discouraged with school. He wants to leave and work on the family farm. His *standardized test scores* are:

- Grade 1, Peabody Picture Vocabulary Test, IQ 145
- Grade 6, Otis Lennon, IQ 140
- Iowa Tests of Basic Skills

	Grade 3 Percentile	Grade 5 Percentile	Grade 7 Percentile
Vocabulary	95	94	98
Reading Comprehension	99	99	99
Language	98	95	98
Work-Study Skills	90	85	90
Arithmetic	95	99	99

His *report card grades* are as follows:

	Grade 3	Grade 5	Grade 7
Reading	A	A	A
Language Arts	A	A	A
Science	A	B	B
Mathematics	A	A	A

Informal inventories yield the following data:

1. *Study Habits.* Andrew kept a weekly log of study and work habits. He did not study any school subject and wrote, "I learned everything in class." He read two library books about animal husbandry and spent thirty hours working on the family farm. Included were five hours entitled "bookkeeping."
2. *Interest Inventory.* In a teacher-prepared interest inventory, Andrew wrote:

I like . . . . . animals.
I dislike . . . . . grade 8 textbooks.
In my spare time . . . . . I am the 4H club president.
My greatest ambition . . . . . is to be a successful farmer.

What do these scores mean? What cautions should you exercise in analyzing these scores? What additional information do you need?

Example 3

Brian, who has just retired from the army, wishes to enter a second profession, preferably in the sciences. He has a B.S. in physics. The following are his *standardized test scores:*

1. Iowa Silent Reading Tests, level 3, Form E[7]

	Raw Score	Standard Score
Test 1: Vocabulary	36	197
Test 2: Reading Comprehension	30	172
Tests 1 and 2: Reading Power	66	185

Included in the test manual is the following information for four-year college and university persons taking the test.

	No. of Items	Mean	Std. Dev.	Std. Error of Mean	Mean	S.D.	Std. Error of Mean
Test 1: Vocabulary	50	28.3	10.6	3.2	181	27	8.1
Test 2: Reading Comprehension	50	32.2	9.7	3.1	179	29	9.2
Tests 1 & 2: Reading Power	100	60.8	19.0	4.7	180	27	6.6

Normative information from the test manual includes the following statement: "A sample selected to be representative of the upper elementary and secondary public school population was defined on the basis of geographic location, size of school district, and a socioeconomic index based on median family income and medium years of schooling of adults in the community." The geographic distribution of the sample participating in the Spring, 1972, research program was:

Area	Percent of Total U.S. Public School Enrollment	Percent of Pupils in Research Program
North Atlantic	24	29
Great Lakes and Plains	28	31
Southeast	22	20
West and Southwest	26	20

2. Wide Range Arithmetic Test II, 90th percentile, norm group was the general population of his age.
3. Minnesota Spatial Relations, 85th percentile, local agency norms.
4. Stanford Binet, IQ 126 (tested when he was a high school senior)

Brian's *college transcripts* are:

• Engineering courses: B + average
• Physics courses: B average
• Humanities courses: A average

Informal tests yield the following information:

1. An informal inventory for one week of spare time activities showed: five hours spent building a stereo set from second-hand components; two hours spent reading a novel; and three hours spent gardening.
2. Previous professional positions include: engineer in the army, ten years; bookkeeper for a small business, three years.

What further knowledge is needed about the test items? Are the norms useful? What other normative information is needed?

Notes

1. *Test Service Bulletin No. 54,* Dec. 1959 (The Psychological Corp.), 3.
2. *Test Service Bulletin No. 36,* Aug. 1948 (The Psychological Corp.).
3. *Test Service Bulletin No. 54,* 3.
4. K. F. Jackson, *The Art of Solving Problems* (New York: St. Martin's Press, 1975).
5. *Peabody Picture Vocabulary Test* (Circle Pines, Minn.: American Guidance Service, Inc., 1959).
6. *Gates McGinitie Reading Readiness Test Kindergarten and Grade 1* (New York: Teachers College Press, Columbia University, 1968).
7. *Iowa Silent Reading Tests, Level 3,* (New York: Harcourt Brace Jovanovich, 1973).

Bibliography

Buros, Oscar K., ed. *Personality Tests and Reviews.* Highland Park, N.J.: Gryphon Press, 1970.

Buros, Oscar K., ed. *Tests in Print.* Vols. 1 and 2. Highland Park, N.J.: Gryphon Press, 1974.

Buros, Oscar K., ed. *The Eighth Mental Measurements Yearbook.* Vols. 1 and 2. Highland Park, N.J.: The Gryphon Press, 1978.

Jackson, K. F. *The Art of Solving Problems.* New York: St. Martin's Press, 1975.

Johnson, Orval G., ed. *Tests and Measurements in Child Development: Handbooks I and II.* Washington, D.C.: Jossey-Bass, 1976.

Tarczan, Constance. *An Educator's Guide to Psychological Tests.* Springfield, Ill.: C. C. Thomas, 1975.

Test Service Bulletin No. 36. The Psychological Corp., Aug. 1948.

Test Service Bulletin No. 54. The Psychological Corp., Dec. 1959.

Woody, Robert H., ed. *Encyclopedia of Clinical Assessment.* Vols. 1 and 2. Washington, D.C.: Jossey-Bass, 1980.

CHAPTER SIX

Writing Techniques for Appraisal Reports

A ppraisal reports are written to record the facts of analysis and to communicate these facts to clients and to professionals involved in the analysis of an individual. For the beginning counselor, report writing may seem a formidable and time-consuming task. However, writing ability develops through practice, by reading the reports others have written, by observing effective models, and by learning the basic rules and structures of writing. This chapter will present the steps in writing an appraisal report, as well as grammatical considerations and ideas for writing with clarity.

Introduction

Writing ability is developed by hard work. Holscher[1] states that "easy writing is hard to read." Writing that is carefully designed, developed, and evaluated is easy to read. The writer must know to whom the report is addressed—a client, supervisor, or colleague. The writer must also know if the report is:

- to be presented orally
- one of a series or stands alone
- a basis for immediate use or is intended for future reference.

Readers desire reports they can understand and that are written in a familiar language pattern. They want information in as concise a form as possible. In counseling, reports usually summarize previous events and are used as vehicles for decision making. Thus, readers wish factors useful in decision making stated clearly. Details of data and extraneous items do not have a place in the body of an appraisal report. They may, however, be placed in an appendix for usage when needed.

The writer must generate a report for the persons who will read and use it. Clients want to know what the report suggests for their futures. They want the most important items delineated clearly. Professionals want to know what the report indicates they must do in helping clients. They want the most important facts backed by reliable data. Thus, the usage of the report by the readers determines the ways in which reports are written and formulated.

Steps in Writing an Appraisal Report

The following steps in writing a report should prove helpful to the beginning counselor.

1. Find out who the readers will be and direct attention toward helping them understand, clearly, the aspects of the report that affect them.
2. Read similar reports already developed in your counseling center or agency. Pattern your report on the approved formats and guidelines of your agency. (Refer to figure 6.1.)
3. Decide upon a point of view. Use either first, second, or third person. Most reports are written in the third person singular.
4. Develop an outline of your report. Write major and minor headings.
5. Using your outline as a guide, generate a rough draft. Work hard. Do not stop writing. Force your pen to keep moving. Write rapidly and include everything that comes to mind.
6. Rewrite each section of your outline. Use all collected data to verify statements.
7. Confer with knowledgeable colleagues and supervisors to be certain that your line of thought is reasonable, compatible, and objective. Change your views to match theirs only if you believe the change is better, useful, and viable.
8. Reread your report. Condense it and rework statements for format, clarity, and brevity. Check for grammatical and stylistic errors.

9. Write all items in order of importance in each category. If possible, place the most important statements first.
10. Write minor headings. Place details under these headings.
11. Reread, condense, rework. Check for technical and grammatical errors.
12. Write conclusions and recommendations.
13. Have colleagues read draft and make comments.
14. Reread. At this point you may wish to alter the outline and revise everything completely.
15. Reread again. Ask yourself these questions: Am I proud of this? Are there gaps in my writing? Are the summary and conclusions consistent with the introduction and data?
16. Place details of data in an appendix.
17. Type a draft copy.
18. Proofread.
19. Type final copy.

Criteria for an Appraisal Report

	Yes	No
1. *Format Items*		
Cover sheet		
Signatures		
Title page		
Table of contents		
List of tables		
List of figures		
Appendix		
Summary		
Conclusions		
Recommendations		
2. *Style*		
Material is in logical order		
Necessary data included		
Written in language of reader		
3. *Grammatical Items*		
Correct spelling		
Correct punctuation		
Clear sentences		
Clear paragraphs		

Style and Grammatical Considerations

In order to write clearly and to convey desired meanings, grammatical errors must be eliminated. Each counselor should know the areas of grammar in which he or she is likely to make errors and should check each report for these errors. The following is a listing of some common errors and stylistic ideas that should be considered.

Agreement

Subjects and verbs should agree. Agreement difficulties may arise when the subject of a sentence is too long. Keep your subject close to the verb.

Anybody

Anybody, anyone, everyone, everybody, and each are singular. So are the verbs that go with them and the pronouns that refer back to them.

Fragments

Check for sentence fragments. Be certain there are a noun and a verb in each sentence.

And here it is! A sentence fragment.
And here is its counterpart—a complete sentence![2]

A clause is not a sentence. If your sentence begins with *when, if, because, although, which, who,* or *that,* it is probably a clause.

If

After *if,* use the subjunctive. Write "if he were," not "if he was"; "if I were," not "if I was."

Infinitives

Keep the two parts of an infinitive verb together, as in "to walk" or "to run." Use "to walk slowly" rather than "to slowly walk."

In that

In that and *due to the fact that* should be avoided. They are vague and show imprecise thinking.

Its and it's

It's equals *it is*.
The possessive of *it* is *its*.
The plural of *it* is *they*.

Misplaced Modifiers

Modifiers attach themselves to nearby words even if the result doesn't make sense. Check modifiers and place them as close as possible to the words they modify. "The patient ran to the counselor, dressed in his birthday suit" should be changed to "The patient, dressed in his birthday suit, ran to the counselor."

Modifiers

Avoid modifiers such as *very, quite,* and *particularly*. They reduce the clarity of meaning. Use "He is a competent workman" rather than "He is a particularly competent workman."

Nouns into verbs

Beware of too many nouns ending in *-tion* and *-ment*. Convert these long nouns into active verbs. Use "John isolated himself from the other patients" rather than "There is a sense of isolation in John's behavior."

One

Avoid too many constructions using *one*. Change *one* to a specific subject or try a term that is less vague, such as *the person* or *the student*.

Parallelism

Each phrase or clause in a series must be written in the same format or parallel structure. "He wants to get out of jail, go to college, and obtain a job in counseling."

Participial Phrases

Watch out for participial phrases! Be certain they modify what you intend them to modify. They should be attached as closely as possible to the part of the sentence they modify. "A participial phrase is a group of words in which what seems to be the verb is in the 'ing' form."[3]

Pronouns

A pronoun refers to something else; therefore, it must agree with its antecedent in number and gender. Watch out for pronouns that agree with more than one nearby noun.

If you have trouble with pronouns, check each sentence that contains *it, he, she, they, that,* and *this.* Then ask yourself the following questions:

1. What is the pronoun's antecedent?
2. Are both the antecedent and the pronoun singular or are both plural?
3. If singular, is the antecedent masculine, feminine, or neuter? Is your pronoun the same?
4. Does the pronoun refer to the nearest noun it agrees with? If not, are you certain its reference is clear?
5. Finally, would each sentence including a pronoun communicate the meaning you have in mind to someone else who does not know you?[4]

Run-on Sentences

If you tend to place too much material in one sentence, read the sentence aloud and place periods where your voice pauses.

Sense

Your writing should make sense to the reader. Parts of writing that do not make sense are usually those parts the writer has not thought out completely. Know what you want to say and say it clearly.

Sentences

Sentences should be concise and direct. Write "Tables 4 and 5 show" instead of "By looking at tables 4 and 5 one can see." Write

"The study of Mary Ann's drug usage showed" instead of "In the study of Mary Ann and her drug usage, it was shown that."

Sentences should be brief. Those over thirty-five words should be broken down into smaller components.

Time and Tense

Be certain that time relationships make sense. Events in the past should be in the past tense and events in the present, in the present tense. "Julian was on drugs in April but at the present time is free from them."

Time sequences of events should be placed in logical order so that the reader is able to make sense of the chronological ordering of events. "Mrs. Belle broke her baby's arm in March and again in June."

Voice

Use the active voice. Write "Several counselors have submitted reports" instead of "Reports have been submitted by several counselors."

Word Usage

Use words that are little, simple, familiar, plain, and precise. For example, write "Please return this book to me after you have read it" instead of "After you have had a chance to peruse this book, return it to me." Use "This made the work easier" rather than "This alleviated the work."[5] Use the usual words of your profession. Read the reports written by others in your institution or agency and use the words that are customary.

Punctuation

Use a comma:

1. Before *and* and *or* in a series of three or more, such as: "the height, width, or depth," "in a study by Thomas, Beck, and Gilbert."
2. To set off a nonessential or nonrestrictive clause, that is, a clause that the sentence can do without. For example: "The switch, which was on a panel, controlled . . ."
3. To separate two independent clauses joined by a conjunction,

especially if the clauses are lengthy. For example: "The floor was covered with cedar shavings, and paper was available for shredding and nest building."

Do not use a comma:

1. Before an essential or restrictive clause, that is, a clause that identifies, limits, or defines the word it modifies. For example: "The switch that stops the recording device also controlled . . ."
2. Between the two parts of a compound predicate. For example: "The results were not in agreement with Smith's hypothesis and indicated that the effect of intervening problems was nonsignificant."

Use a semicolon:

1. To separate two independent clauses that are not joined by a conjunction. For example: "The subjects in the first study were unpaid volunteers; those in the second study were paid for their participation."
2. To separate items that already contain commas. For example: "The color order was red, white, blue; blue, white, red; or white, red, blue."

Use a colon:

1. Before a final phrase or clause that illustrates, extends, or amplifies preceding material (if the final clause is a complete sentence, it begins with a capital letter). For example: "They have agreed on the outcome: Informed subjects perform better than uninformed subjects." "The digits were shown in the following order: 3, 2, 4, 1 in ratios and proportions." "The proportions (salt:water) were 1:8, 1:4, and 1:2."
2. In references between place of publication and publisher. For example: "New York: Wiley, 1958."

Dash

Use the dash only to indicate a sudden interruption in the continuity of a sentence. Overuse weakens the flow of the material. For example: "These two subjects—one from the first group, one from the second—were tested separately."[6]

Proofreader's Marks[7]

Mark in the margin	Mark in typeset text
℘	delete; take it out
⊃	close up; print as one word
℘	delete and close up
⌵ *word*	caret; insert here
#	insert a space
eq. #	space evenly where indicated
stet	let marked text stand as set
tr	transpose; change order the
⊏	⊏ set farther to the left
⊐	set farther to the right ⊐
‖	‖align
⊗	imperfect or broken character
¶	begin a new paragraph
Sp	spell out 5 (set 5 as five)
Cap	set in Capitals
lc	set in Lower Case
Ital.	set in italic
⌄	comma
⊙	period
⌃	semicolon
⌄	apostrophe
⌃	colon
⌄⌄	quotation marks
(/)	parentheses
[/]	brackets

Notes

1. H. Holscher, *How to Organize and Write a Technical Report* (Paterson, N.J.: Littlefield, Adams, 1965), 10.
2. Bryan Reddick, *Effective Writing Style* (New York: Richard Prosen Press, 1976), 97.
3. Ibid., 83.
4. Ibid., Reddick, 97.
5. Holscher, *How to Organize and Write a Technical Report,* 92.
6. *Publication Manual* (Washington, D.C.: American Psychological Assoc., 1983), 53.
7. Ibid., 160.

Bibliography

Holscher, H. *How to Organize and Write a Technical Report.* Paterson, N.J.: Littlefield, Adams, 1965.
Publications Manual. Washington, D.C.: American Psychological Association, 1983.
Reddick, Bryan. *Effective Writing Style.* New York: Richard Prosen Press, 1976.

SECTION THREE

METHODS

AND

MATERIALS

CHAPTER SEVEN

Self-Reporting Devices

There are many nonstandardized test techniques and devices that can be utilized to gather data about clients. Before using a technique, the counselor should consider whether the data gathered will enhance problem solution. Unless the technique adds to relevant data gathering, it should not be used. Not all techniques are suitable for every area of counseling. The counselor needs to know the values of the various techniques and must be able to choose the most appropriate. Chapters 7, 8, and 9 discuss three categories of non-test techniques: Self-Reporting Devices, Staff Reports, and Sociometric Scales. Role playing will be discussed in chapter 13.

Self-reporting devices are forms that contain information the client has given to the counselor. In a self-reporting device a client writes statements or answers questions. These devices rely upon the client's ability to read and write with understanding about the problem being discussed. They include personal data blanks, questionnaires, autobiographies, daily logs and daily plans, sentence completion forms, essays, diaries, life histories, and the device of "write a problem." Before using a self-reporting device, the counselor should consider:

1. What is to be done with the results?
2. What is reliable interpretation?
3. What useful data will be gathered about the client?
4. Is this type of appraisal objective or subjective?
5. Does this type of information show reality?
6. Will the information be of any use in solving the client's problems?

Personal Data Blanks

Personal data blanks have two general functions for the counselor:

1. To gather personal information before the client enters counseling or an institution.
2. To gather information not available from the usual data gathering processes of the institution.

Personal data blanks are essential tools for the counselor. They (1) provide easily obtainable information; (2) are convenient to file and use; and (3) save time. Obtaining the same information by means of an interview is more time consuming.

Personal data blanks may be of any length and may cover areas of personal knowledge such as life history and economic, social, and health status. Personal data blanks should be as brief as possible and clearly worded. Ample room for writing should be provided in the blank spaces, and only information relevant to the problem should be required. The client should be told the reason for needing the information and every attempt should be made to avoid items that would appear threatening to the client. If open-ended questions are used, they should have a definite purpose. For example: ''The names of books I have read recently are . . .'' ''The thing that worries me most about coming here is . . .''

Data blanks should be of a convenient size for filing, such as 3 by 5 inch cards or 8 by 11 inch sheets. If they are to be used for permanent files, they should be reproduced on heavy paper.

Usage in Counseling

In elementary and secondary schools, personal data blanks are used upon entrance into a new school, before interviews, to delineate problems, for health check-ups, before college and career placement interviews, and to gain knowledge about a student that is not available in cumulative records.

In higher education, they are used as noted above and to supplement available college data. They can be used to discover a student's desires and wishes for academic and personal counseling.

In career counseling, blanks may be used before an interview or before career or job searches to delineate strengths, interests, and desires.

With clients who have emotional, criminal, alcohol, and drug problems, the personal data blank should be worded and presented in nonthreatening ways. At times, these clients may be unfit to give information, and personal information will need to be obtained in other ways.

In family counseling, the personal data blank is used in initial interviews, for specified reasons during interviews, and as exit devices. In initial interviews, personal and family histories may be obtained and reasons for the interview stated. As exit devices, personal data blanks may evaluate the interviews and provide for follow-up services.

In counseling the elderly, personal data blanks will serve the same purposes as for previous groups and will depend upon the reason for the counseling service—whether it is for educational counseling, for job placement, or for personal reasons.

From time to time, counselors should reevaluate the ways in which they conduct business and try to develop personal data blanks that will facilitate their work. Well-devised blanks may expedite the fact-finding process and give the counselor more time for helping individuals. For example, I found myself spending up to two hours in interviews with people with degrees who wondered if they should become secondary teachers. They would become upset when they learned about state teacher certification and university requirements. They argued about the requirements and wasted interview time. When they were asked to fill in a personal data blank and match their course work with requirements before the interview, the interviewing time was cut in half. While completing the forms, most of these persons came to conclusions on their own because all the information they needed was on the data blanks. Interviewing time was then based upon more important questions such as, "Do I really want to be a high school teacher?" "What is the high school world really like?" "Will I find a job in my field?"

Examples of Personal Data Blanks

Some examples of personal data blanks developed by counselors follow.

Family Counseling Center

                                                              Exit Form

Name _____ Date _____

Address _____ Phone _____

1. a. In which services of the center would you like to participate?

                                                              Check

        1. Husband-wife counseling   _____
        2. Child-parent counseling   _____
        3. Total family counseling   _____
        4. Assertiveness training classes   _____
        5. Child rearing group sessions   _____
        6. None   _____
        7. Other: Please specify _____

        _____

    b. When would you like these services to begin? _____

2. Of what value were the services in which you have just participated?

    Name or type of service _____ Date _____

    Circle: very effective   helped a little   not effective

    Comments: _____

    _____

3. What other services (not listed above) do you wish the center

    would offer for you? _____

    _____

    _____

    _____

Career Counseling Center

Entrance Form

Name _____Date _____

Address _____Phone _____

Age _____

1. Have you completed High School?   Circle one: Yes   No

   Number of years of college _____

   College major(s) _____

   Degree(s) obtained _____ Year _____

2. List skills for the job market that you now possess:

   a. _____

   b. _____

   c. _____

3. List all jobs or volunteer work you have done: (begin with most recent)
   Job   Full Time   Part Time   Volunteer   Dates

4. What are the major hindrances to the accomplishment of your goals? (check)

   a. Family   _____   e. The job market   _____

   b. Financial   _____   f. Lack of a college degree _____

   c. Care of children   _____   g. Other (please specify)   _____

   d. Lack of H.S. diploma _____   _____

5. Which services of the career center would you like to utilize? (check)

   a. Testing (academic) _____   d. How to get a job seminar _____

   b. Career (testing)   _____   e. Other (please specify)   _____

   c. Individual counseling   _____
       about jobs   _____

Questionnaires

Well-devised questionnaires are among the most useful tools for the counselor. From questionnaires may be obtained basic information about clients and their attitudes, feelings, and beliefs about the effectiveness of programs. Questionnaires are useful when one wishes to gather information which may be obtained by yes-no, multiple choice, or short-answer questions. If a more personalized approach is needed, the interview plus a questionnaire may be used. If clients cannot read or comprehend the meanings of the questions, the usage is limited. In these instances, the counselor should read the questions to the client or translate the sentences into the language patterns needed for comprehension.

How to Write a Questionnaire

Many questionnaires are not answered well because they are too long, badly composed, or lacking in appeal or interest. In counseling, questionnaires must be appealing, interesting, relevant to the client's needs, well composed, at the client's reading level, and designed for ease of tabulation. The format of a questionnaire is dependent upon the reason for the questionnaire, the clients to be served, and the usage of results. Steps to take in writing a questionnaire are:

1.   Define the overall reason or purpose for the questionnaire. For example, in a group session for parents in family counseling, it might be necessary to find out the "basic causes of preschoolers' temper tantrums." This is the overall reason or purpose. Write this as the title of the questionnaire:
"Questionnaire for Parents about Temper Tantrums."

2.   State the major reasons for the questionnaire in a preamble that sets the stage, explains the background, and tells how the questionnaire is to be answered. In complex questionnaires, the preamble might include a brief cover letter or statement explaining the purposes and requesting the client's help in answering the questions. For example, in the questionnaire about temper tantrums, the preamble might be: "Temper tantrums cause difficulties in a home. How may parents learn to help their children? Parents need to find out what happens *before, during,* and *after* a tantrum. This week, write down the sequence of events during one or more temper tantrums."

3.   Write specific questions related to the minor problems to be investigated. These may be arranged in a variety of ways such as true-false questions, multiple choice questions, sentence completion, and essays. In our example, an essay format might be used if parents had developed strong observational abilities. If they were unaware of what was actually happening, true-false, multiple choice, or sentence completion items would direct their thinking about the first minor purpose, "What happens before a tantrum occurs?" Examples of these types of questions are:

True-False Questions:

(Circle)

The tantrum occurred when the child wanted something
he or she could not have   T   F

Multiple Choice:

The tantrum occurred when the child:
(Check)

_____ Wanted something he or she could not have

_____ Was taken away or interrupted in an activity he or she was enjoying

_____ Was tired

_____ Observed or listened to a family happening of which he or she was not a part or could not understand

_____ Other (Describe) _____

Sentence Completion:

The tantrum occurred when _____

Essay Question:

Describe what happened just before the tantrum.

It is easier to answer a series of true-false or multiple choice questions than a mixture of the two. A person's mind-set becomes geared to one type of question, and using several types is confusing. Essay or sentence completion questions should come at the end of a questionnaire, and plenty of room should be left for answers.

4. Place answers to true-false and multiple choice questions on the right side of the page, in boxes, if possible. However, sometimes the left side is more effective, as above. Answers placed on one side of the sheet make tabulation and reading easier.

5. Write in the language and style of the people who will read the questionnaire. Do not use terms or idioms the client will not understand. Be brief. Group similar ideas—such as the minor purposes—together. Use capitals, underlining, and anything else that will make the questionnaire comprehensible. Remember that a brief questionnaire is best.

6. Write directions carefully: "Circle," "List in order of preference 1, 2, 3," and the like.

7. If possible, pretest your questionnaire on a sample population to find out whether the ideas are clear to the reader.

Evaluation of Questionnaires

Care must be taken in interpreting and evaluating the data from questionnaires. Clients are not always truthful and accurate. The most carefully designed questions may be interpreted differently by different people. Data gained should be evaluated and interpreted against the background of all other data gathered about the client. In client-centered data gathering, anonymity is not needed. However, in the sampling and evaluation of larger populations, anonymity will help individuals answer honestly without feeling threatened by the questionnaire.

Usage in Counseling

In elementary and secondary schools, questionnaires are used for initial school entrance and to find facts that are not available to the counselor in the cumulative folder. Sometimes questionnaires are sent home when the counselor needs information that only the home can give. The types and uses of questionnaires are endless and are dependent upon the counselor's needs and creativity.

In higher education, a file of questionnaires to meet many types of counseling problems may be developed. Some of these might be forms for academic counseling needs, dormitory problems, and the like.

In career counseling, questionnaires that list the client's background, history, and career needs will be in constant use; so will those that relate to job placement.

With clients who have emotional and criminal problems, a variety of uses will arise that are similar to the above. In long-term cases, ongoing needs may be met by periodic questionnaires that assess progress in therapy, feelings toward institutionalization, and feelings toward moving into the regular community. These may help the counselor update the individual client's progress.

With clients in alcohol and drug related counseling, questionnaires may be used relating to causes, times of use, types of drugs, effects upon clients physically and emotionally, and feelings of loved ones toward the client.

In family counseling, questionnaires of entrance and exit into counseling and assessment of progress toward problem solutions are useful.

When counseling the elderly, many types of questionnaires may be used. However, the counselor should realize that the elderly may not wish to complete the forms, or they may have vision and hand-coordination problems. The elderly respond well to the personal touch and may dislike questionnaires because they are impersonal. In most instances, counselors of elderly persons should use interviews and record the information themselves.

Autobiographies

Autobiographies have been written by the great and by the humble. Through autobiographies we gain insight into how a person sees himself/herself and his/her life at a particular time in history. An autobiography may be about a total life or a part of that life.

The autobiography, as a data gathering device, is economical. It presents the client and the counselor with a longitudinal picture, and it helps the client with self-assessment. The act of placing one's life on paper may help the client understand the fact and fiction of his or her personal existence. The autobiography is most useful when dealing with personal problems related to self-identity and self-realization, where it is important to put the problem in perspective. It is useful to the counselor because it may show how the client perceives himself, his problems, and his lifestyle. For some clients, the experience of writing or reading an autobiography is traumatic. The counselor needs to be aware of each client's feelings and attitudes toward self-realization.

The autobiography has limitations. The prime limitation is that the act of writing is difficult for many persons. If a person has poor reading and spelling abilities, writing an autobiography is impossible. For such a person, a tape recorder may be used and the transcription typed. Another limitation is that the client may not be truthful and may write a fanciful story. In such cases, the counselor must be able to understand the dynamics of the situation and be able to help the client understand what is happening. The autobiography may help to perpetuate myths the person has built around himself or herself, instead of leading to an understanding of self. The counselor must not take the autobiography at face value, but must evaluate it in terms of the total knowledge gained about the client and the client's problems.

The autobiography may be unstructured or structured. In the unstructured autobiography, the client is asked to write "The Story of My Life" or "What Has Happened to Me" or "How I Feel about My Problem." The unstructured format leaves much latitude for the writer and may or may not cause the gates of personal feelings to open. In the structured autobiography, the counselor may be very definite about the topic, the time frame, and the length. For example, if a counselor were trying to help a boy with a history of stealing to place his life patterns in perspective, he/she might ask the boy to write a structured autobiography as shown in the following example. The purpose would be to bring feelings about himself and his family to a verbal level.

My Autobiography

1. Write your activities at the stated times on the following days:
   Monday, May 30: 4–5 P.M.
   Thursday, June 6: 9–10 P.M.
2. Describe how you felt at 12 P.M. on June 6, when the police came to your home.
3. What did your mother do?
   How do you think she was feeling?
   How do you feel about your mother now?
   How did you feel about her then?
   Do you like the way she feels, now?
   Do you like the way you feel about what happened?

Evaluation

The autobiography is a point of departure for discussions related to self-understanding of behavioral patterns. If untruths or fantasy were shown in the above example, this would be verified by court and police documentation. Through discussion, the boy might be helped to understand that his statements are not factual. In this example, the boy's feelings would be difficult to evaluate, but one could note the type of stated feelings he had had toward his mother and whether he was able to react to the feelings of others. Evaluation of an autobiography is subject to much error and must be seen in light of the facts obtained from a variety of sources.

Some of the things to look for in an autobiography, where feelings are involved, have been listed by M. A. Kiley.[1] These are:

1. *Overall Appearance:* Is it neat and tidy? Is the handwriting coordinated?

2. *Length:* Is there a reason for the length? Structured papers tend to determine length, whereas unstructured depend upon the client's reaction to the assignment.

3. *Language and Semantics:* What is the quality of English and the ability to express oneself?

4. *Quality and Depth of Expression:* The age and educational background of client will show differences. What is the client's attitude toward writing? Toward freedom to express what he [or she] feels?

5. *Tone:* Is there an emotional tone evident such as fear? Is there a specified tone relating to an important event associated with the problem under study? Is this of value to a total understanding of the client?

6. *Gloss, Omissions and Emphasis:* Why do these occur? Is it important that something has been omitted or emphasized? For instance, if a client omits the reasons why he did a certain thing, is this because he doesn't want to face it, or because he has faced the issue and it is irrelevant for him to talk about it anymore.

7. *Distortions, Lies and Unconscious Error:* Is the client writing creatively or is he engaging in fantasy that has a bearing upon the problem? Does the client know he is making an error in fact? Is the omission important to the solution of his problem?

8. *Organization:* Does the client think in a logical manner about the problem? What parts of the autobiography did he place in important positions?

Usage in Counseling

In the elementary school, the autobiography is not used very often up to grades three or four because children find extensive writing difficult. Oral autobiographies may be used in the primary grades and will present the child as he or she is at a certain time and place. Oral and written autobiographies may be used in grades five and six. They may focus on such topics as "Here I Am" and "My Life." Sometimes, an autobiography focused on a problem will be self-revealing to a middle grader: "My Problem is—has been—" or "How I Have Learned to Live with My Problem." These topics give a sense of who I am, plus "I am worthwhile because I can cope."

In high school, the autobiography is sometimes an English assignment, and the teacher and counselor may cooperate in developing and evaluating an instrument for specific purposes. The usage by the counselor is usually on a one-to-one basis with a student who is in a long-term study and is in need of self-assessment and self-understanding. Topics that might arise are: "Why I Can't Hold My Part-Time Jobs," "The History of My Class Assignments," and the like.

In higher education, the autobiographies are used much less than in high school. The long-term associations with a student, which are needed with this device, are less common.

For persons with alcoholic and drug-related problems, autobiographies help clients understand where they have been and where they are going in problem solution. Topics might be "My Life Just Before I Took Drugs," "My Feelings During My Teens and Twenties When I Got Drunk," and so on.

When counseling the elderly, an oral autobiography is often an enjoyable experience. It brings back memories, gives the client a chance to share his/her world with another, and shows the client that his/her life has been productive and worthwhile. It may lead to a sense of accomplishment and the knowledge that one belongs to the society at large. I may help the client know that he/she is one of the survivors, knows how to cope, and is able to live successfully with the problems of old age.

Autobiographies should be evaluated objectively. A counselor must be careful not to read into them more than what is there. The following autobiography has been evaluated by two persons. Subjective comments are underlined. As you read the evaluations, decide how you would evaluate this autobiography.

Anne, age eleven, is having difficulty with math and does not complete her assignments on time. She wrote this autobiography:

> I like school and my teacher is nice. Sometimes she is mean, but not to me. I don't like fractions and I don't like grammar. I was born in New York City, but we moved to California when I was two and then we moved here when I was four. I don't remember living anywhere else but here. My father lived with us in California, but not here. My mother works and she says I'm Joe's little mother. He's seven and has curly red hair. I am supposed to be writing about my life, but not much happens, except going to school and looking after Joe until Mother comes home. Sometimes, we go ice skating and to church and I sing in the church choir and so does my mother. Joe sings in the children's choir. I guess you would say we are a singing family.

> *Evaluation 1* (subjective comments are underlined)
> Anne is a <u>quiet child</u> who <u>has to work very hard at home</u> and <u>has no time for her studies</u>. She <u>misses her father</u> and <u>has little recreation</u> except church activities. Her paper is too short for a sixth grade child, so .he must be <u>hiding something</u>. The paper is <u>poorly organized</u>. She <u>does not have any friends</u>. I would suggest counseling sessions with her mother to see if she can give Anne more free time so that she can have time for friends and her studies.

> *Evaluation 2*
> Anne's paper shows her to be a child who dislikes math and grammar. She has a working mother with whom she shares common interest in skating and singing. She babysits her brother. I do not think this autobiography shows why she is having difficulty with math.

Daily Logs and Daily Plans

Daily logs and daily plans are two facets of the same process. They are used to help clients budget time. When keeping a daily log, a client records the activities at particular times in the day. In the daily plan, a client looks ahead and plans what to do at certain times in a day or week. Daily logs help clients see themselves as they are, whereas daily plans help clients plan changes in behavior according to desired purposes and goals.

The Daily Log

The purpose of the daily log is to help clients understand how they use time. Daily logs also may be used to help clients understand the time frames of behavioral patterns. Some suggestions would be to:

1. Keep a log for twelve hours of your day.
2. Keep a log of the exact times you study without daydreaming. Count the number of minutes you daydream, study, get up and do something else such as waste time, talk, eat, and the like.
3. Keep a log of your feelings from 7 P.M. to 10 P.M. at night. List your feelings as high, average, or low. Describe what caused the fluctuations in your feelings.

Two examples of daily logs follow.

Daily Log 1

My Study Times

Name _____ Date _____

Purpose: To discover how many minutes per day are spent studying.

    Key: * study times

         # daydreaming during study times, times one gets up, walks around, or wastes time

    Directions: On the hour, every hour for two days, write down what you have been doing. Make a red * for each period of study time. Record number of minutes spent in each activity (use key).

Time	Monday	Activity	Tuesday	Activity
7:00 A.M.				
8:00 A.M.				

Daily Log 2

My Hourly Feelings

Name _____ Date _____

Purpose: To discover what activities are associated with high and low feelings.

    Key: * feeling well

         # feeling ordinary

         0 feeling badly

Directions: On the hour, from 7 P.M. to 10 P.M., describe your activities and your feelings. You may have several to record for each hour. Use the key and write down the number of minutes for each feeling e.g.: 35 min. = *; 20 min. = #; 5 min. = 0.

Time	Activity	My Feelings
7:00 P.M.—8:00 P.M.		
8:00 P.M.—9:00 P.M.		
9:00 P.M.—10:00 P.M.		

The Daily Plan

The daily plan may be used to teach a failing college student how to budget time. The student may be directed to: "Plan four hours of study time, with two fifteen-minute breaks. Budget the hours so that your failing subjects are studied first and for the longest periods of time." In family counseling, the daily plan may be used to help a family learn to spend more time together. The parents may decide to plan the hours from 7 to 10 P.M. for six days. During these hours, they will include three hours of family fun, three hours for mother and father to spend together, and one hour each night spent helping children with homework. The plan will arise from mutual family desires and goals developed in conference with the counselor and all family members.

Usage in Counseling

In the elementary school, daily logs and plans may be used in many ways. They can help children learn to study and concentrate. Children can learn how much time they actually spend daydreaming or doing schoolwork. Daily logs and plans can also help the organization of the "latch-key child," who needs to develop a daily time schedule.

In secondary schools and higher education, daily logs and plans are among the most useful and effective tools the counselor may use to help students plan time effectively. Students can learn to budget the hours in a day, including a balance of academic and social activities. These techniques are helpful with students who are failing classwork. Students are able to analyze present daily living patterns and understand how to develop a daily plan that will facilitate efficient study habits.

In family counseling, daily or weekly logs will show spouses the actual amounts of time they spend together. Parents can see the time and quality of their activities with their children. It is an excellent way to bring family members to self-realization about priorities in their lives. Who is most important in your life? What activities do you consider vital to your life style? What time allotments must be changed if the family is to stay together as a unit?

For those with emotional, criminal, alcohol, and drug-related problems, daily logs and plans may be a vital part of rehabilitation planning. Activities may include hourly scheduling, setting goals and purposes for each day, discovering what one's daily time allotments are, and discussing what one needs to do to plan a day that will lead to worthwhile life goals. With strong goal commitments, careful planning, and monitoring of daily plans, clients may be led to modify lifestyles.

When working with the elderly, a flexible daily or weekly plan may be evolved that will give structure and meaning to life. The elderly lose contact with the work-a-day weekly cycle. They need to have flexible plans so that their lives have some structure and they have certain things to look forward to each day and week.

Evaluation of daily logs and plans is dependent upon the client's purposes. If a college student is disorganized, he or she must first desire to change. By means of a log, he or she can find out the circumstances that lead to wasted time, plan an organized day, and learn to follow the plan. The daily log may be used to evaluate the daily plan; the daily plan will be effective only if the client wants to change the findings of the daily log. Both processes complement each other.

Sentence Completion Forms

Sentence Completion Forms are based upon projective techniques that require interpretation by professionals. Therefore, counselors should use and interpret these with caution. Counselors should ask themselves many questions about the results obtained: "Is the answer merely an associated response to the beginning words in the sentence? Is the answer a one-time response? How can I be sure the response is meaningful and related to the problem at hand?" Above all, the counselor must not read more into the replies than is there and must evaluate the replies in the light of all other knowledge gained. For example, if a sentence begins: "I hate . . ." and a child completes the sentence with "my mother," do not believe the child hates the mother. All other evidence must support this view, and the counselor must be cautious when making conclusions.

The sentences in a Sentence Completion Form may be general or specifically oriented to the client's problems. General questions would be:

1. I like _____ .
2. I hate _____ .
3. I am happy when _____ .
4. I never _____ .

Specific questions about study problems might be:

1.   When I study, I feel _____ .
2.   The subject I like best, I study _____ .
3.   I daydream when I study _____ .
4.   I think people who study well and make good grades are ___ .

In elementary schools, children will write what they feel. Insights may be gained into attitudes in many areas. However, attitudes are likely to be fleeting and changeable. In secondary schools and higher education, students will be cautious about filling in the blanks and will tend to write what is thought to be the most favorable response. A rule of thumb for usage should be "Use sentence completion forms when individuals need to express feelings and are not afraid to write down what they are feeling." These forms should be used cautiously with the elderly; those with criminal, drug, and other problems when more data are needed about feelings; and in situations where exposure of feelings will not be a traumatic experience. The technique may be used in long-term counseling with clients about whom considerable data have already been gathered. These forms must be evaluated in light of all knowledge known about a client.

Essays

Written or oral essays about a problem, its inception, or present state may be used with persons who write or express themselves easily. The value is often therapeutic for the writer. When problems are written down, they do not seem so enormous. The act of writing sometimes helps to relieve tensions. Sometimes after writing about a problem, a client will not feel the problem exists anymore. The act of writing will have clarified the issues and placed the problem in perspective. The essay topic should be related to each client's particular problem, such as: "Reasons Why I Have Been Fired" and "What I Dislike About School."

In elementary and secondary schools, the essay is a useful tool to let students get issues "off their chest" and to uncover problems. It is an easy device to use, but evaluation and follow-up are time consuming for teachers and counselors. If the essay is done as part of an English assignment, the teacher might evaluate the English and grammar while the counselor evaluates the problems of particular students. Thus, faculty knowledge is combined on the same project.

In higher education, the process would tend to be time consuming but would be a useful tool when a client in a counseling center needed to express feelings.

In alcoholic, drug related, and career counseling, the amount of usage would vary and would depend upon the particular problem and the particular client.

With emotional and criminal problems, usage might be effective in long-term counseling. If clients wrote essays at various points in time, a series of essays could be placed side by side and progress noted.

With the elderly, essay writing sometimes is enjoyed because there is time to sit, write, and ponder. With others, the writing process is too difficult and the effort is impossible.

The evaluation of an essay is dependent upon the value of the data obtained in relation to the total file of data about the client. A suggested evaluation form follows.

An Essay Evaluation Form

---

1. Has something new been discovered about the problem? Yes No
   a. If "Yes," state items:
   b. Of what value is this knowledge to the problem?
2. Were tensions relieved through the process of writing? Yes No
   How do you know?
3. Is a follow-up interview needed? Yes No
   If "Yes," what are the purposes for the interview?

Diaries

Diaries are daily writings to oneself or to the diary about events in one's life. They are part of the growing-up cultural process of girls between eleven and fourteen years of age. For the young girl in our Western culture who is about to enter womanhood, a diary answers two basic questions: "Who am I?" and "Am I important in the scheme of things?" The first question is answered by the diary which says, to the girl, "You are you. You are special. You are so special that even the tiniest event in your day is worthy of noting within my pages." The diary answers the second question by saying, "You are important, a book is being written about you. Only important people in the history of the world are written about in books."

A diary is secretive. It has a lock and key. It is for the young girl alone. Perhaps a page will be shared with a peer, but the contents will never be shared with those younger or older. It is a place where a young girl can share her deepest and most intimate thoughts with a book. It is a process of self-actualization. It is a process in which the girl turns inward for strength to meet the problems of the day. The act of writing in a diary comes to an abrupt halt when the young girl tries to write about the day's happenings and nothing seems important enough to record. The real world beckons and takes over the girl's life, and the diary is tucked away in the corner of a drawer and is forever lost and forgotten.

A counselor may suggest that a client keep a diary, but unless the ingredients of diary-keeping are within the individual, the keeping of a diary does not have much value. The ingredients for keeping a diary are usually (1) being unsure of the two basic life questions of "Who am I?" and "Am I important?"; (2) a need to work out the answers to life's problems by oneself; (3) the ability to find strength and answers within oneself; (4) living in a life-period of introspection, and not partaking of or fully understanding the adult world of reality. For clients with these factors within their present life style, keeping a diary may do for them what it does for young females. The reason for keeping a diary is to cause people to find places in the adult world and to accept themselves as they are. Some clients will enjoy writing a diary and will keep writing and writing. The counselor should not become discouraged if self-actualization is slow. Some young girls write diaries for two or three years. Some stop in weeks, and others need their daily "talk" with a diary for much longer. The same will be true of all keepers of diaries.

Boys do not tend to write diaries. The needs of a young male in our society do not seem to be met by this form of catharsis. The famous male diarists of literature were not writing the type of diary discussed here.

The counselor should not read or evaluate the contents of a diary unless the client insists. One writes a diary only for oneself. The secretiveness is the special part that diaries play in lives. If effective results are to be obtained, the secret bond between the writer and the diary must not be broken. Evaluation may be through questions such as: "Are you still keeping your diary? Do you like to keep it? How often do you write in it?"

Life Histories

The important events in one's life may be placed on a time line, as in a history book. When the client's basic problems have been specified, the problem's history may be superimposed in different colored inks on the life history. For individuals who have difficulty writing or verbalizing, pictures of the events may be drawn with stick figures. In this way, the client sees the major events in his/her life, observes where problems began, and how they have impinged upon his/her life history. The life history helps to clarify the sequence of events involved in the problem. It may be used with any client who is in need of an understanding of the relationship of a problem to his or her life and to the time sequence of events involved.

The life history may be developed with a client in an interview.

Life History		Problem
1960	Born in Milwaukee	Father drinking
1966	Grade one in Milwaukee	In hospital with broken arm due to father breaking it when drunk
1969	Parents divorced	
1970	Moved to Detroit	Mother drinking
1974	Went to Western H.S.	Client began to drink
1977	Bought first car	In jail for drunken driving
1978	Car accident	Court trial
1980	Married	
1981	Divorced	Drinking heavily
1983	Car accident	In jail

Write a Problem

The techniques of "Write a Problem," "What Is Bothering You?" or "List Your Major Problems" are helpful with clients who need to define, specifically, the major and minor problems affecting their lives adversely. The act of trying to state major and minor problems in order of difficulty will cause the client to clarify thinking, state problems objectively, and eliminate ideas that are not basic to the problem and to problem solution.

Clients should be given time to write problems, or record them on tape. After this is done, the counselor needs to help the client define and clarify the statements. The technique may be used with all clients who are having difficulty analyzing the maze of life factors that may surround the roots of problems. A suggested format for this technique follows.

Write a Problem

A. Write a list of the problems that bother you	B. Check (√) the most troublesome problems of Column 1	C. Underline the *one* that bothers you the most
1.		
2.		
3.		

The "Write a Problem" technique should be used in settings where the client and counselor may discuss the results. The value of this technique is in the give and take of counselor-client discussion.

Notes

1. M. A. Kiley, *Personal and Interpersonal Appraisal Techniques* (Springfield, Ill: C. C. Thomas, 1975), 64–77.

CHAPTER EIGHT

Staff Reports

Staff reports are important in the evaluation of clients' problems. These reports are wide ranging in scope and may be adapted to particular settings. Counselors will develop those that save time and effort and that help gather and record data efficiently. In this chapter, three staff report techniques will be discussed: Observational Reports, Rating Scales, and Cumulative Records.

Observational Reports

Observation is a major means of gathering data and is one of the most used of the non-standardized data-gathering techniques. Although the subjectivity of the processes of observation leaves much to be desired, well thought-out processes and reporting practices help to make the technique more objective. Observations, and the recording of these, may be used to help a client's self-awareness, to provide information for case studies, and to record changing behavior patterns in many counseling settings. Problems include the observer's biases, ability to comprehend what is happening, and ability to take effective notes while observing. Evaluation poses several problems. What do written or taped notes mean? What should be done with an observer's notes? When counselors observe behavior, enough time should be utilized to enable the recording of a client's true behavior patterns. When observation occurs over short periods of time, results should be used with caution.

The Critical Incident Method

The "critical incident" method utilizes observation during a critical incident directly related to the problem being studied. Notes are usually written after the fact because in most situations there is no way of knowing when the incident will occur. Since the writing is done after the incident, the observer will have difficulties recording objectively, especially if he/she were involved in the incident. A second observer, if available, will strengthen the objectivity of the record. When a critical incident is recorded, it should be seen as a single incident, not as a total life pattern. The setting for the incident and what happened before its occurrence should be noted. Two formats for recording critical incidents follow.

Critical Incident Form

Name _____ Date _____

Name of Observer _____

1. The setting. State briefly what happened before the incident. What was the client doing? What were the other persons present doing?
    2. Length of time of incident _____ minutes. Began at _____

    Ended at _____.
    3. Describe the incident (use objective statements only).

    4. What happened afterward? What follow-up treatment was used?
    5. Summarize what happened.

Critical Incident Form 2

Name _____ Date _____

Time of incident: from _____ to _____

Observer _____

Setting _____

Date	Incident	Reaction	Therapy

Comments and Summary:

Running Commentaries about Observations

The observer uses shorthand, a tape recorder, or quick notes to record what is said and done. A secretary may be employed to take the notes and transcribe them. Major and minor incidents may be underlined in colored pencil for ease of summarization. This is an accurate though time consuming and costly method.

Anecdotal Records

An anecdotal record is a written description of an observed event in a client's life. It contains an objective account of actions and verbal statements. Subjective comments may be included in an anecdotal record, but these should be separated from the objective account. The purpose of anecdotal records is to record patterns of behavior that may prove valuable in helping clients solve problems. One or a few anecdotes are not of much value. A series of anecdotal records written over a period of time is needed before patterns of behavior may be documented. More than one observer will help to make the observations more accurate. When a number of anecdotes have been gathered, they may be summarized, and conclusions and recommendations made. The series of anecdotes should be evaluated in conjunction with all other data gathered about the client's problems.

A useful format for many types of anecdotal records is shown.

Anecdotal Record Form

Number of anecdotes to date _____

Name _____**Jane Wing**_____ Age __**2**___ Date __**April 2, 1983**__

Observer: _____**Mrs. Green**_____

Time Observation Began: 4:20 P.M. Time Ended: 4:30 P.M.

Reason for Observation: In play therapy, Jane makes the mother doll hit all the dolls. We would like to know how Jane reacts to her mother, in person.

Setting: (State physical setting, persons present, and activity in which client was engaged.)

Play therapy room with a one-way mirror. Child is playing dolls with counselor and has placed the mother and baby doll in a car. At this point, Jane's mother enters.

Objective Description: Jane looked at her mother, took the dolls out of the car, and looked at the counselor. Counselor: "Let's put the dolls in the car and let them go for a ride." Jane: "No, No, No. No go ride. Stay on floor." Jane did not put dolls in car. She sat holding dolls and looking at counselor.

Subjective Summary of what happened: This is the third time in a week that Jane has stopped playing when her mother entered the room. We are trying to find out why she stops. She put the mother and baby doll in the toy car, but this may be acting out what happens when she leaves here. We do not know why she reacts the way she does.

The subjective section of an anecdotal record must be written with care. The observer should not state personal feelings about the case, or jump to immediate conclusions about the observed behavior such as in the following statement: "I believe Jane hates her mother and I believe that her mother is mean to her." Do not comment on an incident that has created an emotional reaction in the observer until time has elapsed.

In the objective section, record everything verbatim and accurately. It would be better to omit the anecdote than to record one that is inaccurate.

An Observation Checklist

When more than one person is observing, or when one observer writes similar observations several times, a checklist may be used. It is easy to administer but does not provide for the unique happenings of a written observation. Checklists are developed to meet the particular needs of an institution or agency and will vary from setting to setting. A suggested checklist for use when observing a child in a classroom might be as follows.

Classroom Observation Checklist
Topic: Study Habits

Name _____ Date _____ Age _____
Observer _____
Time: from _____ to _____
Classroom Activities at time of observation _____

Check behaviors noted:	Yes	No	Not Observed
1. Listens to teacher			
2. Is courteous to teacher			
3. Is courteous to other children			
4. Works on assignments			
5. Participates in discussions			
6. Uses time efficiently			
7. Understands assignments			
8. Is well organized			
9. Other			

Comments:

When there is a possibility that anecdotal and observational record files may be used in court proceedings, counselors should make themselves knowledgeable about state and local laws. Subjective statements should be omitted or written with care. All statements should be verified by more than one observer.

Evaluation

It is difficult to determine how many anecdotal or observational records are enough. Overuse is a waste of time and effort. A rule of thumb is to collect anecdotes and observational records until the problem is shown with clarity or a point has been reached beyond which any more anecdotes would be redundant.

A series of anecdotes or observation checklists may be evaluated in the following way:

1. Sort the anecdotes into categories such as those that impinge on the problem and those that do not; or sort into specific categories such as attitudes toward others, attitudes toward things, and changes in behavior.
2. Read each category carefully and make a short objective summary of the facts.
3. Write recommendations and conclusions. If possible, have another trained observer repeat the evaluation process.

Usage in Counseling

In early childhood clinics and in elementary schools, anecdotal records and observations are widely used to study child behavior and growth. In high school settings, formal observations and records are difficult, but the counselor-student interview is a type of observation and may be recorded. With other groups, the usage is dependent upon the chance to observe clients in a setting that is meaningful to the problems involved.

Rating Scales

Rating scales list the traits to be observed and present quantitative methods for scoring these traits. They are useful in all areas of counseling. Counselors may develop them when an efficient, quantified means is desired for rating traits commonly observed in a particular situation. In rating clients, counselors should take into consideration the following factors:

1. Observe objectively and be aware of personal biases.
2. Try to avoid the halo effect. When a client rates very high or very low on one important item, there is a tendency to rate the client similarly on all other items.
3. Be cognizant of the tendency to rate clients near the middle of a rating scale. Sometimes when a rater is unsure of the meaning of a rating trait or score, the rating may be placed near the middle. This also happens when the counselor is unwilling to commit himself/herself to a definite positive or negative score. If definitive ratings are not used, the reasons for the middle-of-the-road ratings should be noted.
4. Realize that a personality trait cannot be placed on paper. The rating describes the outward observable manifestation of what is believed to be the trait.
5. Realize that a rating scale in and of itself is useless. It is part of the total data that are gathered about a client's problems.
6. State definite purposes for each rating scale, and define each rating on the scale in terms that are clear to each observer. Each observer must have the same meaning for a rating. This is accomplished by relating each rating to the overall purpose and by stating the meaning of each rating on the scale with clarity.

Quantifying Rating Scales

Quantifying rating scales may be done in three ways: by ''yes-no'' answers, by rating on a numerical scale, and by a progressively scaled method.

Yes-No Quantification

An example of a yes-no rating scale is:

Classroom Behavior

			Circle
The student:			
participates in discussions	Yes	No	Not Observed
completes assignments on time	Yes	No	Not Observed

All of the "yes" checks and "no" checks in the rating scale may be added and the results compared. If the items are of varying importance, total scores will be meaningless. When some scores are weighted more than others, the counselor should understand that weighting is subjective and the evaluation of added scores, doubtful. Unless each item is of equal importance, the wisest way to evaluate is to consider each item separately and in the total context of what is known about the client.

Ratings on a Numerical Scale

Ratings on a numerical scale may be odd or even:

Ratings on a numerical scale may be odd or even:

(Check)	1	2	3	4	5	(odd numbers)
OR						
(Check)	1	2	3	4		(even numbers)

With an odd number of items, ratings tend to fall near the middle; with even numbers, the rater must decide on which side of the center to place each rating. This causes the rater to give definite positive or negative ratings. The numerals by themselves are meaningless unless explained. There are three forms that may be used to explain the meanings of numerical scales. These are defined meanings, defined upper and lower limits, and self-explanatory terms.

1. *Defined meanings.* These explain the exact meaning of each numeral (1,2,3,4,5). For example, defined meanings in a school setting for a rating scale entitled "Usage of Time" might be:

Excellent = The best possible usage of time you have ever observed with a child of this age and grade.

Very good = The very brightest or most efficient children use time in this manner.

Average = This is the way most children of this age use time in school.

Weak = Not as good as average.

Poor = This is one of the worst examples of time usage one would see in a classroom of children of this age and grade. The child wastes time and does not accomplish anything.

2. *Defined upper and lower limits.* This type of rating is used when it is possible to state the upper and lower limits of a trait, but it is difficult to determine the exact placement of intermediary factors. The rater places a check on a continuum between the highest and lowest traits. High and low limits may be on the left or right of the page and the continuum line is usually unbroken. There is a tendency to rate toward the middle with odd-numbered items and on the left or right of the middle point with even-numbered items.

An example for a rating scale about the ''ability to take part in a discussion'' might be:

1.	2.	3.	4.	5.

1. Discusses actively————————————Does not know how to take part in discussion
2. Contributes well to the————————Does not contribute to the discussion
3. Keeps group discussions——————————Wanders away from topic on the topic

3. *Self-explanatory terms.* These terms are self-explanatory and apply when the trait or behavior may be described in particular terms. For example, for a rating scale entitled ''Completes assignments,'' terms might be:

    a. Always
    b. Seldom
    c. Never

A Progressively Scaled Method

A progressively scaled method that may apply to many disciplines is presented in the chart below. Each item is stated in detail and each category is clearly understood. The example is a rating scale used for selecting the most qualified person for a career position. Each numeral notes a progression of qualities from those ''most desired'' to ''least desired.'' Rating 1 contains all desired qualities, rating 2 has fewer desired qualities, rating 3 has an acceptable number of qualities, rating 4 has few desired qualities, and rating 5 is lacking in most of the desired qualities.

Qualifications for Career Position

1. Rate the individual according to the following criteria.

   Criteria

   A. Most desirable
   1. Has master's degree in discipline
   2. Has more than five years experience
   3. Has worked in specialty for at least three years
   4. Has published at least ten articles or books
   5. Has work ability ratings of excellent for two years

   B. Acceptable
   1. Has published books in discipline
   2. Has ability ratings from noted persons in the field
   3. Has administrative statements about abilities
   4. Has been active nationally and locally in discipline
   5. Is conducting research in specialty field.

2. Rate the individual on the rating scale of 1, 2, 3, 4, or 5, using the criteria listed in 1A and 1B.

Rating Scale

(1)	(2)	(3)	(4)	(5)
Meets all criteria of list A and list B	Has 4 of A Has 3 of B	Has 3 of A Has 1 of B	Has 2 of A Has 1 of B	Has 1 of A Has 1 of B
Most Acceptable	Very Acceptable	Acceptable	Not Acceptable	Not Acceptable

Summary

A rating scale should:

a. Give name, date, time, length of time observed, and name of rater.
b. Give setting for observation.
c. Have a carefully delineated statement of meanings of ratings.
d. Have space for comments.
e. Meet purposes for particular rating scale.
f. Be as brief as possible and avoid extraneous words.
g. Be easily marked and tabulated.
h. Contain a method for scoring and tabulation.
i. Have a meaningful title.
j. Have ample space for comments.
k. Be a flexible and ongoing device.
l. Be revised when needed, discarded when no longer useful.
m. Be pre-tested and reevaluated constantly.

Cumulative Records

Cumulative records are a centralized, efficient means of data collection, are found in all sizes and shapes, and are developed for many reasons. They are a physical storage system for all materials that have been gathered about clients or students. They are usually in folder or file form or on a computer disc for easy retrieval and contain all materials related to the client and the client's problems. In academic settings, they contain all historical and academic facts about a student. The design of a cumulative record is dependent upon the type of usage and the date to be gathered. It should meet the ongoing needs of the particular institution. Cumulative records should not become catch-alls for extraneous information such as anecdotal records, observational reports, tests, and the like. These may be housed separately in bulk-type files. Only summaries of these are usually needed in the cumulative record.

Format

The cumulative record should:

1. Have items arranged in order of importance, well spaced, and with room for comments and summaries.
2. Include data such as name, address, phone, employer, reason for referral, date of entrance and exit, home background, academic record, attendance record, scholastic record, employment history, personality characteristics, health record, and so on.
3. Be of durable stock and expandable.
4. Be a size that will fit institutional filing needs.
5. Have clear type.

Care should be taken that all federal, state, and local laws regarding records in educational institutions are followed. In educational institutions, parents and students must be informed about what is included and must be able to look at and challenge the contents. Counselors should obtain copies of all rulings and should follow all guidelines faithfully.

Interpretation

Counselor should interpret cumulative records with care so that:

1. Important factors and relationships are noted.
2. Items affecting a client's problems will be seen within the total framework of knowledge about the client.
3. Test results will be evaluated wisely and not too much importance given to results of individual tests. Instead, patterns of test results over a period of time will be studied.
4. Any biases of persons who have written comments in the cumulative record are realized.
5. The counselor realizes that the record contains only a brief sampling of the individual's life style.
6. Sweeping generalizations about a client are not made. For example if John's scores show IQ: 1978–91, 1983–85, the generalization that "John is not likely to do well because he has low intelligence" should not be used. Objectively, all that can be said is "John's IQ's is 1978 and 1983 were 91 and 85."
7. The counselor does not introduce biases and previous ideas about an individual into a new problem.

Usage in Counseling

In academic settings in elementary schools, high schools, and colleges, the cumulative record is usually housed centrally. Counselors have access to a central file or computerized system and may obtain print-outs for their personal office files. Some uses of cumulative records in academic settings are to gain an overview of a student's background in preparation for an interview; to note strengths and weaknesses in academic areas; to provide essential information for placement, transfer, employment, or college entrance; to show outside-of-school interests, hobbies, and jobs; and to house important data about a student.

In career counseling, the cumulative record shows areas of strength as well as interests. It can be a basis for job interviews or placement in a training program.

CHAPTER NINE

Sociometric Scales

S ociometric scales are used by counselors when working with stable groups of individuals who know each other and have become part of a cohesive group. These devices are an attempt to place the social interrelationships of a group on paper. They show the relationships between persons in a group at a given time in the life of the group. They do not represent permanent relationships.

Sociometric scales to be discussed are the sociogram, social distance scales, the "Guess Who" technique, and choosing actors for a play.

The Sociogram

The sociogram places group interaction patterns in the format of a table or diagram. It is used when trying to find out the interaction patterns of individuals in a group.

How to Develop a Sociogram

Ask a group of persons a question related to interpersonal actions. The question should ask each person to choose another person for some type of activity. For example, in an elementary school classroom, a teacher's question might be: "With whom do you wish to play ball?" The question must be one of intrinsic, immediate value to the group and one which they will answer honestly and readily. Questions should be positive, and anonymity of replies should be safeguarded.

Place the answers received in a circle according to the following:

1. Place those most chosen in the center circle.
2. Place those least chosen in the outer circle.
3. Place those chosen a few times in the other circles.
4. Mark △ for males and ○ for females.

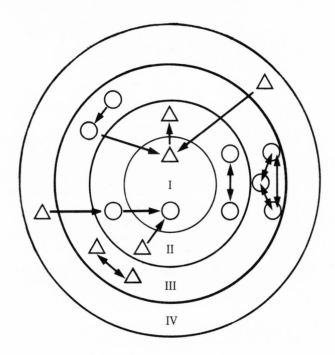

Evaluate the results. Two boys in Circle IV were not chosen but had chosen more popular persons. Two sets of persons in Circle III were grouped together. Circle II had a variety of interaction patterns with individuals in Circle II and with most desired individuals in Circle I.

Sociometric terms that are used to describe the varieties of choice are:

1. Mutual choices ○◄──►○
2. Isolate = no choices received
3. Stars = individuals receiving many choices
4. Clique = a grouping of individuals where each choice does not extend outside the group.

The premise of the sociogram is that individuals will function more effectively if they interact with persons they choose and like. Use the results to help individuals. Look at the isolates and try to find out if being an isolate is a problem. Notice which individuals are mutual choices, stars, or parts of cliques. Evalute the sociogram in relation to the changing patterns of group interaction.

How to Develop a Sociogram with More Than One Choice

The question the counselor asks may be one that has first, second, and third choice answers: "Whom do you wish to invite to your party? Choose three people." The sociogram would be plotted accordingly with first choices receiving a solid joining line _____ ; second choices a line with dashes — — — — — ; and third choice a dotted line . . . . . . For example:

Key:

                              _____ = first choice

     Δ = male   — — — — = second choice

     O = female   . . . . = third choice

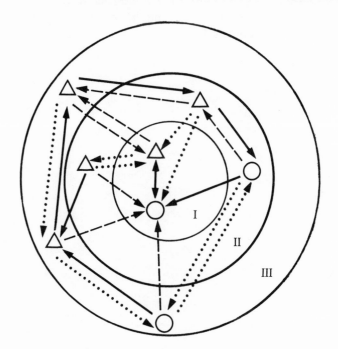

If first choices only were given, it would appear that quite a few persons were isolates. When more than one choice is given, a differing pattern emerges, showing females choosing each other in the top three choices, some males not interacting with females, and everyone being chosen by someone else. Thus, the multiple-answer sociogram may provide the counselor with different interaction patterns than a single-choice sociogram.

How to Develop a Sociogram Using a Table

The sociogram may be plotted on a table. Each person chooses three people he or she would like to have for a friend. The choices are numbered 1, 2, and 3. For example, in the first row, Jean picked Jill as her first choice, Lori second, and Rhonda third. Note that in this sociogram, girls chose girls and boys chose boys. Also, no one chose Bob. In order to clarify the ratings, the numbers of first, second, and third choices are tabulated at the bottom of the sociogram.

In order to clarify the table further, choices may be weighted; a first choice receives a weighting of 3; a second choice, a weighting of 2; and a third choice, a weighting of 1.

Persons Choosing	Jean	Joan	Jill	Rhonda	Lori	Andrew	Jim	Dan	Kevin	Bob
Jean			1	3	2					
Joan	1		2	3						
Jill	1	2		3						
Rhonda		2	1		3					
Lori	1	2	3							
Andrew						1	2	3		
Jim				2	1	3				
Dan			3		1				2	
Kevin					3	1		2		
Bob						2	3	1		

	Jean	Joan	Jill	Rhonda	Lori	Andrew	Jim	Dan	Kevin	Bob
No. of Firsts	3	0	2	0	1	2	1	1	0	0
No. of Seconds	0	3	1	1	1	1	0	2	1	0
No. of Thirds	0	0	1	4	2	1	3	0	1	0
Weighting =	(3 × 3)	(3 × 2)	(2 × 3) (1 × 2) (1 × 1)	(1 × 2) (4 × 1)	(1 × 3) (1 × 2) (2 × 1)	(2 × 3) (1 × 2) (1 × 1)	(1 × 3) (3 × 1)	(1 × 3) (2 × 2)	(1 × 2) (1 × 1)	
	9	6	10	6	7	9	6	7	3	0

Weighting: Third (3) = 1
Second (2) = 2
First (1) = 3

With weighted choices we see that Jill, Jean, and Andrew are stars and Bob is an isolate. Note that this table shows clusters but not mutual choices as effectively as the circle-type sociogram.

Usage in Counseling

The sociogram is most useful in the elementary school. It helps counselors understand group interactions, is an aid in classroom groupings, and helps in the study of group behavioral patterns. Counselors should realize that sociograms show the interaction of students to a certain question at a certain time, but a sociogram does not show causes for the interaction.

In secondary schools and in higher education, the sociogram has few meaningful uses because groups are more fluid. Using one question for placement on a sociogram is too simplistic for the expanding complexities of social interactions at this level.

In career counseling, sociograms are used once in a while to pinpoint persons who may not interact well with others on the job. For instance, in a factory, a stable grouping of employees might be asked ''Which persons do you wish to work with on the assembly line?''

In all other groupings it is rarely used. The exception is in counseling those with emotional problems in institutional settings. Care must be taken so that clients who are labelled isolates do not know the results. For a person struggling for identity and self-actualization, it might be damaging to discover that no one had chosen him for a friend. On the other hand, for a client to discover that he/she had been chosen by many persons might help build self-confidence.

The sociogram is primarily the province of the elementary school. Problems in usage include the amount of time needed to tabulate results, the vagueness of the categories, and the subjectivity of interpretation. Because workable groups are so important in the elementary school, the technique is a very useful tool for counselors as well as teachers.

Social Distance Scales

Social distance scales endeavor to determine the degree, or amount of distance, a client may be away from acceptance by the social group of which he/she is part. The degrees of distance away from acceptance are devised according to criteria considered of value to the particular social setting. Social distance scales may be damaging to the client's self-perception; therefore, discretion is needed in use and in interpretation. As with other sociometric devices, social distance scales do not tell why an individual is accepted or rejected in a particular social setting.

Social distance scales should be used in social groupings where the group has been stable over a period of time. Each member should have the emotional stability necessary to make valid judgments in the area to be rated. Counselors should realize that group opinions may not be of value to the life style and problem-solving ability of the individual involved. Results show the thinking of the respondents and their attitudes toward an individual, but they do not necessarily show a true picture about the individual who was rated. However, social distance scales may be used to find the thinking, likes and dislikes, and prejudices of the group that does the rating. In most ratings, an individual will be liked by someone. This may be used postively in counseling.

Methods for Use

Decide the reason for use of the scale. List all members of the group on one axis of the scale and your criteria on the second axis. Ask each member of the group to check, on a scale, his or her opinion of each of the others according to the stated criteria. Two social distance scores are obtained: a self-social distance score showing what each individual thinks of each member of the group, and a group score showing the actual acceptance or rejection of each member by the group. Finally, evaluate the results.

Examples of Social Distance Scales

Social Distance Scale 1.

Whom Do I Like?

Beside your own name in columns 1, 2, 3, and 4 write the names of persons in the group whom you like, who like you, who like you a little, or who do not like you.

Name	1. People I like	2. People who like me	3. People who like me a little	4. People who do not like me
John				
Jean				
etc.				

Social Distance Scale 2.

Who Are My Friends?

Beside your own name, write the names of persons in the group who think you are their best friend, a friend, a casual acquaintance, or someone they talk to occasionally.

Name	Best Friend	A Friend	Casual Acquaintance	Talk to Occasionally
John				
Jean				
etc.				

A social distance scale may be used to understand the difference between a client's belief and a group's belief about the client's social acceptance. For example, if ten persons checked Social Distance Scale 1, the comparison of a client's rating (A) and the group's rating (B) might be tabulated as follows. Note that the client believes four people do not like him, whereas only one person feels this way.

	A *(Client's Rating)*	B *(Group's Rating of Client)*
	Number of replies	Number of replies
1. People I like	2	
2. People who like me	4	7
3. People who like me a little	2	2
4. People who do not like me	4	1

Usage in Counseling

In group settings and for specified purposes with clients who are being evaluated in many ways over a period of time, the scales may prove useful. Evaluation should compare clients' beliefs with reality. Evaluation may also assess changing social patterns and add to a body of knowledge that is being gathered about a client.

The "Guess Who" Technique

In the "Guess Who" technique, individuals in a stablized group list the names of individuals within the group who best fit the stated descriptions. The results provide the counselor with added knowledge about how a client is perceived by those in the group. Individuals in the group should have the expertise necessary to evaluate others in the area to be rated. This includes the emotional stability necessary to rate others objectively.

Method

State the specific purpose. For example, the purpose might be to find which persons in the group help the group to function well. Then write a stem statement, followed by several possible items, as shown in the following example.

Guess Who?

Write the names of the persons in your group who best fit the following descriptions:
1. Tries to keep group discussions on topic in a pleasant way.
   Name_____
2. Tries to keep the group from fighting.
   Name_____
3. Tries to keep group happy.
   Name_____
4. Tries to help group members who do not know what to say.
   Name_____

Usage in Counseling

Results should be used with caution. The counselor should understand the interpersonal dynamics of the group and utilize the results in ways that will help the client grow in self-understanding. The technique is of value in those settings where a group of clients know each other well, such as in institutions or out-patient clinics where clients meet each other frequently over a period of time.

Choosing Actors for a Play

The technique of "Choosing Actors for a Play" may be used with clients who belong to a stable group and know each other well. Children, especially, respond to this technique because they like to be chosen for parts in plays as long as the parts are not characterized as good or bad, and acceptable or unacceptable. This technique should be used as follows:

1. Know the purposes for using the technique. For example, in a fifth grade class, the purpose might be to discover which students are considered by the class as capable of being strong or funny or weak or wise. Students not chosen for any role should be noted.

2. List the names of the characters with a brief description of their roles.
3. Ask students to write the names of one or more students who might be able to play the part of each character.
4. Note choices and non-choices.
5. Realize that evaluation of this technique is subjective, but that some insights may be obtained into group behavior, beliefs, and attitudes.

Bibliography

E. S. Bogardus. "Measuring Social Distance," *Journal of Applied Sociology,* 9 (1925), 299–308.

Cunningham, Ruth. *Understanding Group Behavior of Boys and Girls.* New York: Bureau of Publications, Teachers' College, Columbia University, 1951.

CHAPTER TEN

Models of Counseling I

F rom the many theoretical models of counseling, this chapter presents short discussions of those that are most likely to be used by the counselors to whom this book is addressed. Therapies and theories developed for clients with severe problems are not included. Included are outlines of behavioral counseling, reality counseling, person-centered counseling, play therapy, and existential counseling. A separate chapter is devoted to transactional analysis. From these the counselor may choose appropriate ways to help clients with problems.

Behavioral Counseling

Behavioral counseling explains behavior in terms of learning and develops behavioral change based upon the principles of learning. It is believed that behavior is learned and therefore may be changed or unlearned. Behavioral counseling relies upon the techniques of classical conditioning. The premise of behavior modification counseling is that problems arise due to negative environments in one's life and the problems may be modified or changed when clients learn desirable behaviors by means of conditioning. These theories have been applied in many settings and have proved effective with groups of persons living in closed settings such as schools or institutions as well as with individual clients.

In behavior modification counseling, observable goals are established and behavior is modified by socially oriented conditioning techniques in which the client learns to change behavior in positive ways. Progress toward goals is evaluated periodically so that the technique can be changed if it does not help the client. The counselor is an active agent in this process. Once the client agrees to the changes to be made, the counselor helps in every way. Each step of the process is explained to the client. Clients are not considered inept or weak. They are shown that learning new behaviors is possible and will enhance their lives. The emphasis is upon learning how to live and how to behave successfully in the present. The counselor learns to know the client, gain rapport, analyze problems, assess the ways in which behavior has been learned, develop goals for change, and make plans for problem solutions.[1]

Several behavioral techniques enable clients to change behavior. Behavior may be changed by reducing the client's anxiety and/or fear. For example, anxiety may be reduced by gradually introducing the client to his or her problem in progressive steps.[2] For example, Mary Ann became upset if her father criticized her appearance. A list of persons who had criticized her from the most disturbing to the least disturbing was recorded: father, brother, best friend, neighbor, and gas station attendant. Mary Ann was taught a relaxation technique; she was told to feel as she did on a happy holiday lying on the beach. She practiced feeling this way until she could relax readily. The criticism least bothersome was stated to her at the same time as she was doing the relaxation exercise. This was repeated until the criticism no longer bothered her. The process was repeated with each of the disturbing criticisms until even her father's criticism was no longer threatening to her. Thus the client learned to modify her behavior through a conditioning process in which she learned to change her behavior in positive ways.

Fear may sometimes be reduced when the client listens to the counselor describe a fear-producing event. If the description upsets the client, the counselor keeps talking about the situation in greater and greater detail. For some clients, the fear is gradually lessened as it is brought into a nonthreatening real-life setting. This technique is sometimes effective when the counselor accompanies the client to a threatening setting in order to help the client realize gradually lessening fears.[3]

Behavior modification may occur when thinking patterns are changed. One technique that has been used successfully in assertiveness training with women helps the client learn that a human being has the right to express thoughts and feelings as long as the rights and dignity of others are maintained. Expressions of love, sympathy, anger, and frustration are appropriate. The client states the areas in which interpersonal problems arise. Role playing is utilized to develop skills in interaction with others. The client practices these skills in simulated and real-life situations and records personal feelings and the reactions of others. Clients are helped to understand that their feelings of inadequacy or frustration are caused by their inappropriate behavior in dealing with others. Through practice in simulated settings clients learn to express feelings to others.

Another technique relies upon the belief that changed thoughts and changed speaking patterns will change feelings and behavior. Clients list the negative statements they make about themselves, others, and their environment. Then they list alternative positive statements. Through role playing and discussions, clients are encouraged to utilize the alternative statements. For example, in a family counseling case, the husband knows his wife will leave him if he doesn't change his behavior toward her. The wife has stated that his dinner table behavior is more than she can tolerate. His statements for one meal are listed and alternate responses chosen. Through role playing, the client is encouraged to develop new verbal statements and in so doing to change his feelings and behaviors toward his wife:

Husband's statements:

1. Where is my tea? I want it *now*!
2. Can't you even remember to put spoons on the table?
3. This steak tastes like leather—just like your mother's steaks. So what can I expect?
4. The sugar bowl hasn't got a lid. Whoever heard of a sugar bowl without a lid!
5. You are the worst cook in the United States.

Appropriate alternatives:

1. May I have some tea when you have time?
2. Will you please give me a spoon?
3. This steak is good.

4. When I go to the store, I'll try to find a lid for the sugar bowl.

5. You are a good cook.

Reality Counseling

Reality counseling or therapy developed from the works of William Glasser and applies to individuals with behavioral and emotional problems. The theory of reality counseling is based upon the belief that each person is personally responsible for his or her behavior and mental health. Responsibility in reality therapy is defined as ''the ability to fulfill one's needs and to do so in a way that does not deprive others of their ability to fulfill their needs.''[4] The system of ideas developed by Glasser is based upon the development of personal identity and responsibility for one's behavior. The value of teaching clients to behave in better ways in order to develop attitudes of success and self-worth is stressed. In reality counseling, the relationship between counselor and client is personal, and the counselor may talk about his/her own personal life if this will help the client. However, the professional role of the counselor is retained, and the counselor does not become entangled in the client's problems.

The counselor leads the client to focus on present problems, and past problems are discussed only if they help alleviate present problems. The counselor's focus in discussions is on behavior, not on feelings. Feelings do not have a place in reality counseling, because this type of counseling is based upon behavioral changes that will solve problems. Through discussion, the counselor brings the client to value judgments about present behavior. Behavior is considered the cause of present problems and failures. The counselor brings present behavior into focus by helping the client face the morality of present actions through defining his or her beliefs about the morality of actions. ''Simple learning theory notions are . . . applied. Behaviors which are sought'' are reinforced ''positively; those which are troublesome are reinforced negatively.''[5]

In order to resolve behavioral problems, a plan of action is formulated by the counselor and client together. This plan is in minute detail and may be developed in small hour-by-hour behavioral steps. The plan is placed in writing, and the full cooperation of the client must be obtained if changed behavior is to be attained. The counselor helps the client accept the reality of the plan by emphasizing ''reality and present behavior.''[6] No excuses are accepted for plans that are not carried out. The counselor focuses on the belief that change in behavior is possible and that plans can and must be carried out. In reality therapy, the goal is development of the client's self-identity as that of a person who can control behavior and be morally responsible for personal actions.

Person-Centered Counseling

Person-centered counseling is based upon the ideas of Carl Rogers, who believed that clients could learn to cope with their environments successfully and in so doing could realize their fullest potential. Rogers believed that the individual is a "self-doer" and develops a self-structure that consists of values received from or taken over from other people.[7]

In person-centered counseling, the counselor's role is to help the client toward self-actualization by being a person who relates in caring, nonjudgmental ways to the client. The counselor should be perceived by the client as someone who believes the client is able to solve problems. The counselor helps the client understand the reality of problems by accepting and understanding the client completely. The client learns to look inward for problem solutions and finds that personal resources are the source of problem solutions. The counselor does not pose as an expert; instead, the counselor is a helper.

Play Therapy

In play therapy, a child is allowed to play out the negative feelings that may be preventing the development of a positive, happy way of life. Play therapy is based upon the belief that play is the natural way that a child learns to solve problems and to understand the environment. Through play, a child learns about life and play acts the solutions to problems.

In play therapy, the child is placed in an environment where objects, such as dolls, are used symbolically. For example, mother and father dolls may be used with children having problems with parents. These dolls symbolize to the child the real parents. The counselor shows interest in the playing but makes no value judgments and merely encourages the child in play. The counselor may reflect the child's apparent feelings by stating, "You are angry with the mother doll . . . ," or "You are angry with the baby doll . . ." If the child responds, the counselor makes no judgments. The child is allowed to play in a free environment where all that is said is accepted. Thus the counselor becomes a sounding board and a person to whom feelings may be expressed freely.

Existential Counseling

Existential counseling has arisen from the philosophies of the existential writers and is based upon helping the client to find freedom of thought. This freedom is an inward freedom in which the individual develops the inner personal power to take a stand despite the external environment, which may not be sympathetic to an individual's inner beliefs.

Existential counseling is concerned with helping a client discover the meaning of his or her particular life. It is believed that behavior stems from the individual's view of his or her place or role in the world. The counselor believes that the client has unlimited potential for growth and this is developed by discussion with others so that the client understands his or her own meaningful relationship to others. Clients are encouraged to understand and to verbalize personal goals and values and to place these in the life scheme of things. The client is helped to focus on self-awareness in the present. Past history is not emphasized. Discussions of anxiety areas of life, such as death, are encouraged so that the client sees the processes of life in a normal perspective. Frey and Heslet (1975) state that the client

> learns to accept himself for what he is and to accept his weaknesses, take responsibility for error.
>
> views life as an unfinished process that is not totally understandable, and sees himself living in this ongoing ambiguous continuum.
>
> becomes aware of and trusts the unchangeable aspects of his personality, yet remaining open to those things he can alter.
>
> becomes relatively free from external expectations and is not defined by theoretical or practical constraints.
>
> views the end of counseling as a challenge to live in a complex world where conflict is real. The client does not seek a calm and issueless existence.
>
> learns to see things as they are, not needing elaborate systems for self-protection.
>
> gives up his self-centered existence and puts himself at the disposal of the demands of life.
>
> views himself with respect.[8]

In existential counseling, change takes place by employing a variety of procedures that focus on one's feelings and on what is going on inside oneself physically and emotionally. Clients are taught to relax, to be silent, to focus thought on inner feelings, and then to verbalize these feelings. The result is a bodily release and a feeling of change as the person is at peace with him- or herself. The client has a feeling of being right with the self and of understanding the self in the context of the total environment.

Notes

1. Earl E. White and Hazel I. Smith, *A Guide to Behavior Modification* (Palo Alto, Cal.: Peek Publications, 1973).

2. Garth J. Blackham and Adolph Silberman, *Modification of Child Behavior* (Belmont, Cal.: Wadsworth, 1971), 53.

3. Ibid., 23,24.

4. William Glasser, *Reality Therapy* (New York: Harper and Row, 1965), xv.

5. Ibid., 130.

6. Ibid., 138.

7. Carlton E. Beck, *Philosophical Guidelines for Counseling* (Dubuque, Iowa: Wm. C. Brown, 1966), 166.

8. David H. Frey and Frederick E. Heslet, *Existential Theory for Counselors* (Boston, Mass.: Houghton Mifflin, 1975), 39–43.

Bibliography

Beck, Carlton E. *Philosophical Guidelines for Counseling.* Dubuque, Iowa: Wm. C. Brown, 1966.

Blackham, Garth J., and Adolph Silberman. *Modification of Child Behavior.* Belmont, Cal.: Wadsworth, 1971.

Frey, David H., and Frederick E. Heslet. *Existential Theory for Counselors.* Boston, Mass.: Houghton Mifflin, 1975.

Glasser, William. *Reality Therapy.* New York: Harper and Row, 1965.

White, Earl E. and Hazel I. Smith. *A Guide to Behavior Modification.* Palo Alto, Cal.: Peek Publications, 1973.

CHAPTER ELEVEN

Models of Counseling II

Counselors need to become aware of the personality transactions occurring between themselves and clients and between clients and others. An interesting way to do this is through an understanding of Transactional Analysis (TA), a counseling theory described by Eric Berne in *Games People Play* and developed by Thomas Harris in *I'm OK— You're OK,* and Jongeward and James in *Winning with People.* Dr. Berne developed his theory as he

> watched behavioral changes in a patient which took place . . . when a new stimulus such as a word, gesture or sound was introduced. These changes included different facial expressions, body movements, and physical gestures. It was as though the individual had several different people inside; at any given time, one or the other of the "people" inside dominated the individual's thoughts and behavior. . . .
>
> Different selves of an individual transacted with other people in different ways and . . . these personal transactions could be objectively studied. . . . Some of the behavioral transactions had ulterior motives; the individual used them as a means of manipulating others into psychological games. [1]

Three Ego States

Transactional Analysis (TA) theory assumes that within each person are three persons—a Parent, an Adult, and a Child (PAC)—or three ego states. These ego states have consistent patterns of behavior that have been recorded and stored in the brain. These patterns of behavior are replayed when a person is in similar situations to a previous setting. The three ego states are described by Jongeward and James (1973) as follows:

> The Parent ego state contains the attitudes and behavior incorporated from external sources, primarily parents. Outwardly, it is often expressed toward others in prejudicial, critical, and nurturing behavior. Inwardly, it is experienced as old Parental messages which continue to influence the inner child.
>
> The Adult ego state is not related to a person's age. It is oriented to current reality and the objective gathering of information. It is organized, adaptable, intelligent and functions by testing reality, estimating probabilities, and computing dispassionately.
>
> The Child ego state contains all the impulses that come naturally to an infant. It also contains the recordings of his early experiences, how he responded to them, and the "positions" he took about himself and others. It is expressed as "old" (archaic) behavior from childhood.
>
> When you are acting, thinking, feeling, as you observed your parents to be doing, you are in your Parent ego state.
>
> When you are feeling and acting as you did when you were a child, you are in your Child ego state.[2]

Meyer (1975) stated:

> The goal of TA therapy is to teach the client to cognitively and emotionally recognize his ego states of Parent, Adult and Child and to help him learn about the basic life position he has assumed in his relationship with other people. It is the client's responsibility to decide whether or not he wants to change his basic life position. As the individual analyzes his transactions, he can gain a more conscious control of how he affects others and how they seek to change him.[3]

The counselor may help the client become aware of the ego state being used in personal relationships. For example, Mary, thirty-eight, has entered counseling with the purpose of developing a changed life style. She understands the principles of TA but has not applied them to herself. She uses the Adult and Child state most of the time. The counselor would like her to be more aware of her usage of the Child ego state.

In the following interview, the discussion centers around Mary's decision to give up her job of many years and to try a variety of jobs. She wishes to find out what type of work she would really like. Beside each of Mary's statements is a C for the Child ego state or an A for the Adult ego state.

MARY: What a mess I'm in! I've given up my job and now I don't know what I want. (A)

COUNSELOR: How did you like your part-time job as a receptionist in the old folks home?

MARY: Oh—those old fuddy-duddies. (C)

COUNSELOR: You did not like the old people?

MARY: Not the ones who came down the hall and told me about their operations! (A)

COUNSELOR: How did you like being a Kelly girl and going out to different firms to type?

MARY: Boring. It's "type this, do that." I don't like being ordered around. (A)

COUNSELOR: Maybe these jobs are not for you.

MARY: You said it! (C)

COUNSELOR: In our discussion, so far you have been using a number of TA ego states. Could you analyze what you have been doing? Are there more productive responses?

Strokes

One term used in Transactional Analysis (TA) that may be utilized by the counselor to expedite human relations is "stroking." In counseling, this takes the form of verbal approval or praise. The receiver of the strokes feels happy and satisfied. In TA theory, stroking may be positive or negative. The theory states that everyone needs some kind of stroking, either positive or negative. Positive strokes develop emotionally healthy persons with a sense of "OK-ness." "The lack of sufficient strokes always has a detrimental effect on people."[4] Effective counselors are often those who know how to give clients positive strokes and who comprehend the problems involved by the negative strokes a client receives.

Life Positions

In TA theory, it is believed that individuals utilize one of four attitudinal ways of thinking about others. These are (1) a positive attitude toward others and one's self, (2) a positive attitude toward one's self and a negative attitude toward others, (3) a negative attitude toward one's self and a positive attitude toward others, and (4) a negative attitude toward one's self and others. It is important for the counselor to realize which basic attitude toward self and others the client employs in daily interactions with others and which attitudes a client employs when interacting. Attitudes other than the positive attitude toward one's self and others will cause problems for counselor and client in interpersonal communications.[5]

Games

Through an understanding of TA, the counselor may gain further understandings of the dynamics of interpersonal relationships operating during contacts with clients. In TA theory, an individual develops a personalized script, or game, which matches the self-image that the individual is endeavoring to convey to others. These psychological games have hidden messages, or purposes, intended for the receiver. These games are repetitive and are played in order to win out over the other person. These games prevent honest and open relationships between people. Meyer stated that, "People play them because they provoke attention, reinforce early opinions about others, and reinforce their thoughts about their own basic life positions."[6]

Jongeward and James listed three basic elements in the psychological games people play. These are:

1. A series of complementary transactions, which on the surface seem plausible.
2. An ulterior transaction, which is the hidden agenda.
3. A negative payoff, which concludes the game and is the real payoff.[7]

These elements may be illustrated by the game of "Kick Me." In this game, the player does something to provoke another player. "A person who is used to the game of 'Kick Me' tends to attract others who can play the complementary hand and are willing to 'kick' him."[8] For example, a client might say to his wife, "I stayed at work too late last night and was unable to bring home the groceries." The wife replies, "Well, I'll have to get them myself because you are unreliable." Thus the individual's action seems plausible on the surface, but the hidden agenda is to find someone who will kick him and prove to him that he is worthless.

Some other games described by Jongeward and James are:

1. Harried. An individual says yes to everything and acts out the game until collapse or depression is justified.
2. See What You Made Me Do. Instead of taking responsibility for his actions, the individual plays a game that proves that personal faults are caused by others.
3. Lunch Bag. In this game, an individual uses a self-righteous position to manipulate others. This person may make an issue of eating lunch at work and avoid other's demands by making them feel guilty to approach such a busy person.
4. Stupid. In this game, an individual "accidentally" does something stupid in order to prove stupidity.
5. Wooden Leg. Nothing much can be demanded of the individual because he or she has a handicap.
6. Now I've Got You. The individual catches another making a mistake and makes him pay for his mistake.
7. See How Hard I Tried. The individual can't be blamed for things going wrong because he or she tried so hard.[9]

In the following interview, the counselor's purpose is to help Mary learn how to control the games she plays with others.

COUNSELOR: Good morning. You look so attractive in that blue dress.
MARY: Thank you. I'm glad you like it, but it doesn't do too much for me, do you think?
COUNSELOR: I really like it.
MARY: Well, you are most likely mistaken. My brother just looked at it and said, "Some dress!"
COUNSELOR: What do you think he meant?
MARY: I've no idea. He's brutally honest with me, and you are just trying to be kind. So I guess it looks awful on me—especially the color. This shade of blue makes my face look too pale.
COUNSELOR: Mary, what kind of game are you trying to play with me?
MARY: (laughing) I want you to tell me this dress looks terrible on me, but you won't cooperate, and I know the next question you will ask is "why." I know why. I want you to reinforce what my family believes.
COUNSELOR: This game has taken up interview time. What might have been a more efficient way to have structured this time period?
MARY: I could have accepted your compliment and not played a game.

COUNSELOR: What could you do to learn how to accept compliments?

MARY: I did say thank you, but then I didn't leave it at that. Maybe I should leave the conversation at "thank you." Isn't it strange how I play "Kick Me"?

COUNSELOR: Why did you play "Kick Me" today?

MARY: I was angry with my brother for glaring at my beautiful dress and not complimenting me.

COUNSELOR: Why do you think he refuses to give you compliments?

MARY: He doesn't know how, and he has never really liked me.

COUNSELOR: What must you do so that he doesn't affect your inner feelings about yourself?

Types of Transactions

TA theory describes the transactions people use in interpersonal relations in the following ways:

1. Complementary transactions are ones in which people are on the same wavelength. Messages that are sent from one person to another get an expected response, and the lines of communication are open.
2. Crossed transactions are those in which messages sent from one person to another get an unexpected response. People withdraw from each other or the conversation goes in another direction.
3. Ulterior transactions have a double message because the hidden agenda is more important to the sender and to the receiver than the stated verbal message.[10]

The counselor may help clients learn to keep the lines of communication open by explaining the basic types of transactions and helping the client analyze transactions. For example, in the case of Mary, she is open and communicative most of the time but uses ulterior transactions with hidden meanings. The counselor doesn't always know what she is trying to do to the conversation. As the counselor carried on the following interview, it appeared that Mary was putting the counselor down to reinforce her belief that others were not OK.

MARY: You know, you make things clear to me most of the time, but when it gets right down to the crux of the matter, you are unable to follow through and help me.

COUNSELOR: I don't really understand what you mean.

MARY: That's what I'm talking about. As a counselor, you lack understanding of the basics—you are a person who leaves out basics. For example, look at this end table for client use. It doesn't have a sharpened pencil or an eraser for clients to use in filling out these forms. You're weak in basics.

COUNSELOR: I think you are giving me two or three messages, and I do not know which is the one you are intending me to receive.

MARY: (in disgust) That's what I mean, you don't understand basics.

COUNSELOR: You are trying to tell me that I'm not OK as a counselor and as a person.

MARY: Oh no, I don't mean that.

COUNSELOR: Do you feel better when you tell me I'm not OK? Do you understand why you broke into the discussion with a putdown of me?

MARY: I'm not trying to put you down . . .

Summary

Some clients may be aided in the discussion of problems if they understand the three ego states of Parent, Child, and Adult, and the reasons people play games rather than communicate openly and honestly with others. The counselor's awareness of TA games will prevent the counselor from being manipulated by game-playing clients and will enable the counselor to help clients realize the reasons for their use of manipulative games. To be effective, problem solution must be conducted in an open, honestly communicative environment in which a client is able to look at problems objectively and observe personal actions with clarity. The counselor may help the client identify the games and roles being played and learn ways to eliminate these from daily living. This may be done by discussion, role playing, and noting the interpersonal methods utilized by the client in an interview.

Notes

1. James B. Meyer and Joyce K. Meyer, *Counseling Psychology* (Boston, Mass.: Allyn and Bacon, 1975), 97.

2. Dorothy Jongeward and Muriel James, *Winning with People* (Menlo Park, Cal.: *Addison Wesley*, 1973), 19.

3. Meyer and Meyer, *Counseling Psychology,* 103.

4. Jongeward and James, *Winning with People,* 60.

5. Thomas Harris, *I'm OK—You're OK: A Practical Guide to Transactional Analyses* (New York: Harper and Row, 1969).

6. Meyer and Meyer, *Counseling Psychology,* 102.

7. Jongeward and James, *Winning with People,* 73.

8. Ibid., 75.

9. Ibid., 73–76.

10. Ibid., 44.

CHAPTER TWELVE

Ethical and Legal Considerations in Counseling

The counselor should be familiar with the ethical standards of the particular professional organization to which he or she belongs, as well as the legal considerations that affect counseling as stated by federal, state, and local governments. Within these regulations and standards, each agency or counseling center should develop guidelines to meet local needs. Legal standards safeguard clients and counselors in areas of behavior where individual and local mores may be wanting. Ethical guidelines cause counselors to scrutinize personal standards of behavior toward others. It is to be expected that counselors will have high personal standards in human relationships, but attention to defined standards will enhance each counselor's behavior toward clients.

Ethical Standards of Professional Organizations

The ethical standards of the American Personnel and Guidance Association, the National Education Association, and the American Psychological Association have clear statements regarding the counselor's role in the analysis of the individual. The following statements show that high ethical standards are expected of members in the dissemination of information about clients, the confidentiality of information, and the maintenance of the client's welfare. The American Personnel and Guidance Association's *Ethical Standards* state:

Section A: General

8. In the counseling relationship the counselor is aware of the intimacy of the relationship and maintains respect for the client and avoids engaging in activities that seek to meet the counselor's personal needs at the expense of that client. Through awareness of the negative impact of both racial and sexual stereotyping and discrimination, the counselor guards the individual rights and personal dignity of the client in the counseling relationship.

Section B: Counseling Relationship

1. The member's *primary* obligation is to respect the integrity and promote the welfare of the client(s), whether the client(s) is (are) assisted individually or in a group relationship. In a group setting, the member is also responsible for taking reasonable precaution(s) to protect individuals from physical and/or psychological trauma resulting from interaction within the group.

2. The counseling relationship and information resulting therefrom be kept confidential, consistent with the obligations of the member as a professional person. In a group counseling setting, the counselor must set a norm of confidentiality regarding all group participants' disclosures.

5. Records of the counseling relationship, including interview notes, test data, correspondence, tape recordings, and other documents, are to be considered professional information for use in counseling and they should not be considered a part of the records of the institution or agency in which the counselor is employed unless specified by state statute or regulation. Revelation to others of counseling material must occur only upon the expressed consent of the client.

7. The member must inform the client of the purposes, goals, techniques, rules of procedure and limitations that may affect the relationship at or before the time that the counseling relationship is entered.

8. The member must screen prospective group participants, especially when the emphasis is upon self-understanding and growth through self-disclosure. The member must maintain an awareness of the group participants' compatibility throughout the life of the group.

Section C: Measurement and Evaluation

The primary purpose of educational and psychological testing is to provide descriptive measures that are objective and interpretable in either comparative or absolute terms. The member must recognize the need to interpret the statements that follow as applying to the whole range of appraisal techniques including test and nontest data. Test results constitute only one of a variety of pertinent sources of information for personnel, guidance, and counseling decisions. . . .

1.   The member must provide specific orientation or information to the examinee(s) prior to and following the test administration so that the results of testing may be placed in proper perspective with other relevant factors. In so doing, the member must recognize the effects of socioeconomic, ethnic and cultural factors on test scores. It is the member's professional responsibility to use additional unvalidated information carefully in modifying interpretation of the test results.

2.   In selecting tests for use in a given situation or with a particular client, the member must consider carefully the specific validity, reliability, and appropriateness of the test(s). General validity, reliability and the like may be questioned legally as well as ethically when tests are used for vocational and educational selection, placement, or counseling.

3.   When making any statements to the public about tests and testing, the member must give accurate information and avoid false claims and misconceptions. Special efforts are often required to avoid unwarranted connotations of such terms as IQ and grade equivalent scores.

4.   Different tests demand different levels of competence for administration, scoring, and interpretation. Members must recognize the limits of their competence and perform only those functions for which they are prepared.

5.   Tests must be administered under the same conditions that were established in their standardization. When tests are not administered under standard conditions or when unusual behavior or irregularities occur during the testing session, those conditions must be noted and the results designated as invalid or of questionable validity. Unsupervised or inadequately supervised test-taking, such as the use of tests through the mails, is considered unethical. On the other hand, the use of instruments that are so designed or standardized to be self-administered and self-scored, such as interest inventories, is to be encouraged.

6.   The meaningfulness of test results used in personnel, guidance, and counseling functions generally depends on the examinee's unfamiliarity with the specific items on the test. Any prior coaching or dissemination of the test materials can invalidate test results. Therefore, test security is one of the professional obligations of the member. Conditions that produce most favorable test results must be made known to the examinee.

7.   The purpose of testing and the explicit use of the results must be made known to the examinee prior to testing. The counselor must ensure that instrument limitations are not exceeded and that periodic review and / or retesting are made to prevent client stereotyping.

8.   The examinee's welfare and explicit prior understanding must be the criteria for determining the recipients of the test results. The member must see that specific interpretation accompanies any release of individual or group test data. The interpretation of test data must be related to the examinee's particular concerns.

9. The member must be cautious when interpreting the results of research instruments possessing insufficient technical data. The specific purposes for the use of such instruments must be stated explicitly to examinees.

10. The member must proceed with caution when attempting to evaluate and interpret the performance of minority group members or other persons who are not represented in the norm group on which the instrument was standardized.[1]

The Code of Ethics of the Education Profession adopted by the 1975 NEA Representative Assembly states:

The educator, believing in the worth and dignity of each human being, recognizes the supreme importance of truth, devotion to excellence, and the nurture of democratic principles. Essential to these goals is the protection of freedom to learn and to teach and the guarantee of equal educational opportunity for all. The educator accepts the responsibility to adhere to the highest ethical standards.

Principle 1—Commitment to the Student

The educator strives to help each student realize his or her potential as a worthy and effective member of society. The educator therefore works to stimulate the spirit of inquiry, the acquisition of knowledge and understanding, and the thoughtful formulation of worthy goals.

In fulfillment of the obligation to the student, the educator—

1. Shall not unreasonably restrain the student from independent action in the pursuit of learning.
2. Shall not unreasonably deny the student access to varying points of view.
3. Shall not deliberately suppress or distort subject matter relevant to the student's progress.
4. Shall make reasonable effort to protect the student from conditions harmful to learning or to health and safety.
5. Shall not intentionally expose the student to embarrassment or disparagement.
6. Shall not on the basis of race, color, creed, sex, national origin, marital status, political or religious beliefs, family, social or cultural background, or sexual orientation unfairly:
   a. Exclude any student from participation in any program
   b. Deny benefits to any student
   c. Grant any advantage to any student

7. Shall not use professional relationships with students for private advantage.
8. Shall not disclose information about students obtained in the course of professional service, unless disclosure serves a compelling professional purpose or is required by law.[2]

The American Psychological Association's Ethical Principles of Psychologists state:

Principle 1
Responsibility

In providing services, psychologists maintain the highest standards of their profession. They accept responsibility for the consequences of their acts and make every effort to ensure that their services are used appropriately.

f. As practitioners, psychologists know that they bear a heavy social responsibility because their recommendations and professional actions may alter the lives of others. They are alert to personal, social, organizational, financial, or political situations and pressures that might lead to misuse of their influence.

Principle 2
Competence

d. Psychologists recognize differences among people, such as those that may be associated with age, sex, socioeconomic, and ethnic backgrounds. When necessary, they obtain training, experience, or counsel to assure competent service or research relating to such persons.

Principle 3
Moral and Legal Standards

c. In their professional roles, psychologists avoid any action that will violate or diminish the legal and civil rights of clients or of others who may be affected by their actions.

Principle 5
Confidentiality

Psychologists have a primary obligation to respect the confidentiality of information obtained from persons in the course of their work as psychologists. They reveal such information to others only with the consent of the person or the person's legal representative, except in those unusual circumstances in which not to do so would result in clear danger to the person or to others. Where appropriate, psychologists inform their clients of the legal limits of confidentiality.

a. Information obtained in clinical or consulting relationships, or evaluative data concerning children, students, employees, and others, is discussed only for professional purposes and only with persons clearly concerned with the case. Written and oral reports present only data germane to the purposes of the evaluation, and every effort is made to avoid undue invasion of privacy.

c. Psychologists make provisions for maintaining confidentiality in the storage and disposal of records.

d. When working with minors or other persons who are unable to give voluntary, informed consent, psychologists take special care to protect these persons' best interests.

Principle 6
Welfare of the Consumer

Psychologists respect the integrity and protect the welfare of the people and groups with whom they work. When conflicts of interest arise between clients and psychologists' employing institutions, psychologists clarify the nature and direction of their loyalties and responsibilities and keep all parties informed of their commitments. Psychologists fully inform consumers as to the purpose and nature of an evaluative, treatment, educational, or training procedure.

Principle 8
Assessment Techniques

In the development, publication, and utilization of psychological assessment techniques, psychologists make every effort to promote the welfare and best interests of the client. They guard against the misuse of assessment results. They respect the client's right to know the results, the interpretations made, and the bases for their conclusions and recommendations. Psychologists make every effort to maintain the security of tests and other assessment techniques within limits of legal mandates. They strive to ensure the appropriate use of assessment techniques by others.

a. In using assessment techniques, psychologists respect the right of clients to have full explanations of the nature and purpose of the techniques in language the clients can understand, unless an explicit exception to this right has been agreed upon in advance. When the explanations are to be provided by others, psychologists establish procedures for ensuring the adequacy of these explanations.

c. In reporting assessment results, psychologists indicate any reservations that exist regarding validity or reliability because of the circumstances of the assessment or the inappropriateness of the norms for the person tested. Psychologists strive to ensure that the results of assessments and their interpretations are not misused by others.

d.   Psychologists recognize that assessment results may become obsolete. They make every effort to avoid and prevent the misuse of obsolete measures.[3]

The Counselor's Personal Relationship to the Codes

The codes involve the counselor, personally, in a number of issues. These are:

1.   How may the counselor learn about the codes and laws? This is done through careful reading of the materials endorsed by the counselor's professional organization, by reading the organizational journals, and by attendance at local and national conventions.

2.   How may a counselor present the professional standards of conduct to clients? The Bible says, "By their fruits ye shall know them."[4] A counselor's conduct toward clients will show the professional standards in which the counselor believes. The codes framed and on display in an office will enhance understandings, as will clearly written statements of policy about confidentiality and usage of tests and test results prepared for clients.

3.   How may a counselor internalize the values and social issues involved? As one works in counseling, one meets with questionable happenings. To be prepared emotionally and intellectually for these eventualities, each counselor should review codes and laws, note where there are areas that do not seem important in one's personal scheme of living, and then reevaluate one's value system. In the areas where the counselor believes the issues are of little concern, much personal caution is needed because each individual has to learn to rise to higher planes, professionally, than one does in daily living patterns. For each counselor, the pitfalls of true professionalism are different. For some, a bribe means nothing; for others, a stray word of gossip about confidential matters seems perfectly all right. Therefore each counselor needs to strive towards an individually higher plane of ethics that supercedes personal living patterns.

4.   How may a counselor uphold the highest ethical behaviors when fellow professionals may not be so inclined? To "blow the whis-

tle'' on unethical behavior is a path very few persons have the inner strength and fortitude to follow. This is especially difficult when one's job may be dependent upon silence. Yet, the value of the counseling profession to the public is dependent upon the personal trustworthiness of each counselor in day-to-day working relationships. Each counselor needs to note possible problems before they arise, bring these to the fore, and try to resolve the issues openly and with clarity. In times of crisis, each counselor's true integrity will be dependent upon how the smaller, ethical actions have been handled and how much one's inner strength and integrity have developed.

Laws and Federal Guidelines

During the past ten years, several important laws have been passed to protect the public in areas related to counseling. Detailed knowledge of these laws and their effect on the counseling process may be obtained from specialized courses and readings. However, if a counselor needs to go to court because of some infraction of the law in professional duties, legal counsel should be sought. Fischer and Schimmel (1982) state:

> With many different governmental units creating law and with various courts adjudicating cases, the task of ''finding the law'' can be very complicated. A little knowledge in this instance may indeed be dangerous. . . . Consequently, it is wise to seek counsel from legal aid and legal services, or a private lawyer.[5]

This section discusses counselor immunity before the law, management of student's scholastic records, the Equal Employment Guidelines, and laws about answers to standardized tests.

Counselor Immunity

The counselor has no ''general immunity from the dictates of the criminal law.''[6] Because counseling is a new profession, there have been few court decisions, and so far there is not the body of established laws for the delineation of standards as found in lawyer-client and doctor-patient relations. Yet, as professionals, counselors are expected to respect all legal standards and laws when dealing with clients.

Several states now accord the privilege against testifying in a court of law to the counselor-client relationship. In such states, however, problems may develop about confidentiality in group situations. In states where counselor-client confidentiality does not apply, clients should be told that if called as a witness before a court hearing, the counselor may be required to repeat what has been told. "This is true, no matter how damaging such disclosures may be to the counselor's relationship with a particular individual. . . . It may seem unfair . . . but that is the position of the law at the present time in the majority of states."[7] Burgum and Anderson (1975), referring to group counseling, state that "until present laws are changed, the counselor would be well advised to avoid discussion of criminal acts in group sessions unless the . . . counselees are willing to continue with the knowledge that no confidential relationship exists."[8]

The Management of Students' Scholastic Records

Counselors in schools and colleges need to become knowledgeable about local, state, and federal guidelines related to the management of students' scholastic records. These guidelines protect the family's and the student's rights to knowledge about school records. These laws are enforced by the federal government withholding federal money for school programs where students eighteen or over and parents are denied access to the stated records. The Buckley Amendment to the Family Educational Rights and Privacy Act of 1974 states that parents have the right

> to inspect and review any and all official records, files, and data directly related to their children, including all material that is incorporated into each student's cumulative record folder, and intended for school use to be available to parties outside the school or school system, and specifically including, but not necessarily limited to identifying data, academic work completed, level of achievement (grades, standardized achievement test scores), attendance data, scores on standardized intelligence, aptitude, and psychological tests, interest inventory results, health data, family background information, teacher and counselor ratings and observations, and verified reports of serious or recurrent behavior patterns.[9]

Thus the Family Educational Rights and Privacy Act protects "the confidentiality of school records, it guarantees parents or guardians access to their child's records, and it provides fair procedures to challenge questionable information contained in records."[10]

Employment Selection Procedures

For counselors in career counseling, a knowledge of the Guidelines on Employment Selection Procedures developed by the Equal Employment Opportunities Commission (EEOC) is necessary. These guidelines require that all employers, governmental or private, must demonstrate the validity of their selection procedures. The employer may not impose a requirement that is not relevant to the job.

> The guidelines in this part are based on the belief that properly validated and standardized employee selection procedures can significantly contribute to the implementation of non-discriminatory personnel policies, as required. . . . It is also recognized that professionally developed tests, when used in conjunction with other tools of personnel assessment and complemented by sound programs of job design, may significantly aid in the development and maintenance of an efficient work force and, indeed, aid in the utilization and conservation of human resources generally. . . . Evidence of a test's validity should consist of empirical data demonstrating that the test is predictive of, or significantly correlated with, important elements of work behavior which comprise or are relevant to the job or jobs for which candidates are being evaluated.[11]

For counselors testing clients or preparing clients to take tests, the federal guidelines should be known and understood.

Other sources of federal acts related to counseling are: *Title 20, United States Code,* Section 1232g; *Federal Register,* June 17, 1976, "Final Rule on Education Records"; *Title 20, United States Code* 706, Section 612 (P.L. 94-142); *Federal Register,* August 23, 1977 (P.L. 94-142); and Section 504—1973 *Vocational Rehabilitation Act.*

Answers to Standardized Tests

Due to growing demands by consumer groups for truth-in-testing laws and civil rights groups' complaints about cultural biases in questions on standardized tests, the first state law about these matters was passed in New York State in 1979. This law requires "sponsors of higher admission tests to provide students, on request, with copies of the test questions, correct answers, and their own answer sheets."[12] On July 30, 1980, amendments to this truth-in-testing law were signed. The following are the major provisions of the amendments:

To exempt low-volume Tests administered to less than two thousand test subjects annually from disclosure.

Achievement tests . . . must now be disclosed once every three years.

Test companies will be allowed to administer as many as 5,000 or 5 percent of their tests, whichever is less, on an nondisclosed basis. (This provision is needed because the small population served by these special tests makes the ''requirement to disclose'' in these cases burdensome.)

At least one disclosed test be administered annually for Saturday Sabbath observers and that alternate Sunday tests be offered with the same frequency as regular administrations.

Test agencies will be required to state the median correlation between test scores and all variables whenever the range of correlations are reported in the information materials provided to students.[13]

As more states and Congress become involved in truth-in-testing laws, school and college counselors should be aware of current regulations and advise their students accordingly.

Notes

1. *Ethical Standards* (Falls Church, Va.: American Personnel and Guidance Association, 1981).

2. *Code of Ethics.* (Washington, D.C.: National Education Association, 1974).

3. ''Ethical Principles of Psychologists,'' *American Psychologist,* 36:6 (June 1981).

4. Matthew 7:16.

5. Louis Fischer and David Schimmel, *The Rights of Students and Teachers* (New York: Harper and Row, 1982), 419.

6. T. Burgum and S. Anderson, *The Counselor and the Law* (Falls Church, Va.: American Personnel and Guidance Association Press, 1975), 7.

7. Ibid., 15.

8. Ibid., 23.

9. Buckley Amendment, Family Educational Rights and Privacy Act, Federal Government, 1974.

10. Fischer and Schimmel, *Rights of Students,* 346.

11. *Federal Register,* 35:149 (Aug. 1, 1970), 12333–36.

12. *The Testing Digest,* fall 1980 (New York: The Committee for Fair and Open Testing, 1980), 8.

13. Ibid.

Bibliography

Buckley Amendment/Family Educational Rights and Privacy Act of 1974; Educational Amendments Act of 1974. Washington, D.C.: Federal Register.

Code of Ethics. Washington, D.C.: National Education Association, 1974.

Burgum, T., and Anderson, S. *The Counselor and the Law.* Falls Church, Va.: American Personnel and Guidance Association Press, 1975.

Ethical Standards. Falls Church, Va.: American Personnel and Guidance Association, 1981.

"Ethical Principles of Psychologists." *American Psychologist,* 36, no. 6 (June 1981).

Fischer, Louis, and Schimmel, David. *The Rights of Students and Teachers.* New York: Harper and Row, 1982.

"Guidelines on Employment Selection Procedures." *Federal Register,* 35, no. 149 (Aug. 1, 1970), 12333–36.

Huckens, Wesley. *Ethical and Legal Considerations in Guidance.* Boston, Mass.: Houghton Mifflin, 1968.

Nygaard, Joseph M. *The Counselor and Student: Legal Rights.* Boston, Mass.: Houghton Mifflin, 1973.

Schimmel, David, and Louis Fischer. *The Civil Rights of Students.* New York: Harper and Row, 1975.

The Testing Digest, Fall 1980. New York: Committee for Fair and Open Testing, 1980.

SECTION FOUR

PRACTICAL

APPLICATIONS

OF ANALYSIS

CHAPTER THIRTEEN

Role-Playing Practice

In order to develop skills in the analysis of problems, counselors need simulated practice through role playing. This chapter presents the methods, uses, and evaluation procedures in role playing as well as starter parts for role playing for counselors in elementary schools, secondary schools, and colleges; for those counseling families, the elderly, and persons with criminal and emotional problems; and for those in career counseling.

Role Playing

Role playing is a much used method in counseling today. Values to the participant include:

1. Observing the viewpoint of others.
2. Viewing oneself as seen by others.
3. Acting out one's frustrations.
4. Reaching toward reality by playing real life roles.
5. Forgetting oneself in the action of the play so that personal problems and difficulties are lost for the moments of the acting.
6. Enjoying the spirit of group togetherness.
7. Learning how to become part of the interaction between a group of people.

8. Gaining insights into methods of problem solving as developed by group and individual actions about the play-acted problems.
9. Learning appropriate roles and the expectations of society by watching others act as well as acting oneself.
10. Losing one's fears and inhibitions about taking on new life styles while role playing new life styles.

Role playing is many things to many people. When well conducted and when about topics participants understand, role playing engenders a high level of approval and belief that real learning about the solutions to problems is taking place. Role playing may be used by counselors with clients to solve problems or by a group of counselors to develop their own counseling skills. In this chapter, suggestions are given for simulated practice through role playing to help counselors develop their skills.

Methods of Role Playing

The participants should:

1. Have a commonality of interest. For example, a group of women returning to the job market will have similar goals and will be able to learn from each other.

2. Be diverse enough in personalities to engender conflict. Effective role playing must have conflict. When choosing individuals for roles, the counselor should make certain that at least one person on each side of the conflict is verbal and dominant enough to keep the action moving.

3. Have the necessary background to be able to undertake the assigned role. If a person is given a role completely diverse from any life style encountered, role playing may not be effective.

The role-playing problem should be thought out carefully beforehand, be about a topic of common interest and knowledge to the participants, and have possible conflicts inherent within it. It should also have opportunities for the development of colorful characters, have an element of surprise worked into it, and be about something the participants would like to know more about or might encounter in the future. Furthermore, it should be a learning experience for the participants, with areas of knowledge about which the participants do not know solutions but about which it is possible to find solutions. It could include areas about which the counselor or some other professional is able to give insights. The problem should be one with which the group may identify. The design should be such that the problem-solving aspects carry beyond the period of role playing and cause participants to become actively involved in the discussion beyond the role-playing hour. When this happens, problem solving activity enters the world of reality and becomes part of daily experiences.

When beginning a role-playing session with persons who have never acted before, the counselor should explain that:

1. The play acting will be about common problems and the group will try to seek a group solution.

2. Each participant will have a turn with some role. If a participant cannot think of anything to say, the rest of the group will believe that quietness is the role and will try to solve the problem.

3. Each participant will be given an outline of the character to be portrayed. At first, participants should follow the stated role characteristics. Once the role playing is under way, participants should improvise and try to create the role as the action moves along. They should think about what the character would say and do in real life, and act accordingly.

4. The counselor may, from time to time, give the participants slips of paper with written suggestions as to what a participant might say or do in order to keep the action moving. The counselor should do this only when the action seems to be coming to a standstill and the participants have run out of ideas. If at all possible, participants should be encouraged to think of ways to keep the action moving without help from the counselor.

5. Participants should not worry if another actor gets angry or upset with them. This will be part of the role the person is playing.

In preparation for the role-playing activities, the counselor should write out the parts each person will take. Give one or two persons leading roles and give one participant the problem to be solved. This participant should explain the problem to several key members of the group at the initiation of the action so that the play will have focus. However, some participants will not be told the problem, due to their unique roles. Note that the participants listed below as number 2, Mrs. Jean Jones, and number 3, Bill Jones, are not told the problem initially. The problem needs to be a surprise to them, if they are to react naturally. In this example, Mary Jones is pregnant and afraid to tell her mother and father.

The counselor in charge of the role playing prepares three slips of paper, one for each participant.

Setting: A high school counseling office
Characters:

1. *Mary Jones.* You are fifteen and pregnant. Explain how you feel about this to the group. You do not want an abortion, but do not know what to do. You know you must tell your mother and father. Think of what you will say. You have just decided to tell your mother when you are doing the dishes together at night. (Note: Do not let the other characters hear what you say to the group, this must be a surprise for them.)

2. *Mrs. Jean Jones.* You have a loving husband Bill Jones, and a daughter, Mary, age fifteen, whom you love very much. Mary has a boyfriend, Tom, whom you do not like. He has not been around lately, and you hope Mary has dropped him.

3. *Bill Jones.* You have a wife, Jean, and a fifteen-year-old daughter Mary. You work as a stock man in an auto mechanics store. You work hard to provide a good home for your wife and daughter. You believe it is best, in bringing up children, to be very strict and teach them to obey. Mary has always obeyed you, and you are pleased she is doing well in high school.

4. *School counselor.* Mary has come to see you, and she is in tears.

Initial Role Playing: Counselor and Mary Jones.

Note that each participant has been told something that the others do not know. The pregnancy will be a surprise to participants 2 and 3, just as in real life. If at first participants 2 and 3 do not know what to say, let other members of the group suggest what should be said. With the setting as described, conflict is inevitable; suspense will arise from the participants themselves.

The counselor must be ready at all times to help a flagging participant. Suppose participant 3 does not know what to say and is really at a loss. The counselor may take another group member aside and suggest, "You are John Field, a man who works with Bill Jones. Your daughter was pregnant, and you found the right solution. You took her out of school, and when she had her baby, you saw to it that the baby was adopted. You did not let your daughter go back to school; instead, you found her a job as a salesclerk in a store. You believe an education should not be given to a girl who disgraces her parents." Now suggest that Bill Jones talk to John Field. From this encounter, the role playing should move from the stalemated position.

In preservice counselor role playing, participants, observers, and the counselor in charge of the role playing will want to discuss what has happened. The observers will not agree, necessarily, with the participants. Thus, role playing should be followed by much discussion about what should have been done with the problem.

When using role playing in real-life counseling settings, the counselor should be cautious about participants who are upset by their roles or who find the reality of role playing too traumatic for them. The counselor must know each participant well as an individual and introduce role playing or particular conflicts in role playing when the participant is able to profit from the experience. Sometimes an individual will be helped by watching others and, though unable to perform, will be able to comment on the acting. Sometimes, after a group has become proficient in role playing, they will want to talk about problems and possible solutions rather than to role play. This should be encouraged when skills in role playing are well developed and abilities in problem solving are becoming advanced.

Usage in Counseling

In the elementary and secondary schools, role playing is used in academic disciplines where moods, feelings, and understandings of others are desired. For example, in a social studies lesson, students might role play what women did in various aspects of the westward movement. In an economics class, students might role play the ways in which a family learns to budget income. Up to fourth or fifth grade, children love role playing, and they learn to solve problems in a play-acting atmosphere. After fifth grade, students may be reluctant to role play unless they understand the reasons for role playing and discover the enjoyment of the action.

At the collegiate level, role playing will be enjoyed by groups of young people. It is a useful tool in group sessions where students wish practical ideas and knowledge about the problems of dating, getting along with peers, and preparing for careers.

In career counseling, role playing may be used in group career sessions where persons need knowledge and practice in job interviews and problems such as how to get along with other workers on a job.

In counseling sessions for those with emotional or criminal problems, role playing may include the actions approved by society or problems encountered in family living, work rules, dress codes, and the like.

For those with drug and alcohol related problems, role playing may encompass many topics. Role-playing designs may be based upon questions such as, "Is it better to go through the hassle of getting up in the morning and going to work or staying home and taking a drug? Is it better to go into the bar on the way home at night rather than going home to the noise of the kids?" These may be acted and the alternatives discussed.

In counseling the elderly, acting new roles may help clients understand that they can solve the problems of aging such as fears of hospital stays, and the problems of living with inlaws or living alone.

Evaluation

Role playing may be assessed individually or in group sessions. Many times assessment is not needed, because the role-playing action shows whether the players have resolved conflicts and used reliable problem-solving techniques. If individuals in the group wish to evaluate their own reactions and how they perceived the actions of others, group discussions and/or individual interviews may be used. Sometimes a questionnaire such as the following will prove useful.

Role Playing Questionnaire

Check the following:

1. I learned:____very much____an average amount____not very much about the solution of today's problem.
2. I played my role: ____well____average____did not understand it.
3. I agree with the solution of today's problem. Yes   No

   Why _____.
4. In today's role playing, I wish _____
   _____
   _____

The counselor should assess the value of role playing for each client based upon the reasons for participation in the particular role. Did the client understand the role? Was the client able to indentify with the role? What was the quality of the problem solution? Is the client growing in problem solving abilities?

Role-Playing Designs

The following role-playing designs are examples of possible situations that may be encountered in counseling. Other designs may be developed to meet the role-playing needs of participants. These designs may be used in counselor training in order to develop the skills of participant, observer, and counselor in charge of role playing. Counselors in training should become adept as participants and observers before they take the role of counselor in charge of role playing.

The roles should be modified and changed to suit developing needs of the action. The role-playing action may be video taped, audio taped, or played to a student audience. In each case, observer feedback is important. Sessions related to a problem of particular interest or importance may continue over several days with different groups of participants interpreting problem solutions in different ways.

For Elementary School Counselors

Play 1

Setting: An elementary school on the edge of a large industrial park. Trucks roar by the school and one of the children's major interests is watching people at work in the factories. Many of the children are streetwise. The homes are single family, blue collar, and well cared for.

Characters:

1. *Miss Green.* You are a young first grade teacher and have no idea how to change the thinking and acting patterns of Tom and Bill. Each day brings you more of their problems. A week ago they put gravel in the gas tanks of the cars in the faculty parking lot. Today you have been summoned to the principal's office.

2. *Mr. Vansant.* You are the principal. Two police officers have come to your office to report that last night Tom and Bill, six-year-olds in Miss Green's room, poured gasoline over a cat, set fire to it, and sent

the cat running through an industrial complex. You are infuriated with Miss Green, who is supposed to stand at the corner and watch the two boys until they turn into their own driveways.

3. *Police Officer 1:* You have seen the damage done to the industrial building by the fire.

4. *Police Officer 2:* You have spoken many times to Tom and Bill, their parents, and Miss Green. You believe little progress is being made in the homes. Bill's mother doesn't seem to care. Tom's mother has spent time in jail for theft and encourages Tom in thievery.

5. *School Counselor.* You are responsible for two schools bordering on the industrial park and have had little time to talk to the two boys.

Initial role playing: Principal, Miss Green, Police Officers, and Counselor; meeting is held in the principal's office.

Play 2

Setting: Peter, age ten, in third grade, has been playing truant for most of September and October.

Characters:

1. *Peter.* You are ten years old. You do not like school. You are in third grade and all your friends are in the fourth and fifth grades. Your family moves around the country frequently and you have missed many months of school. You have failed every grade and you are sure you will do poorly again. You believe there is no sense in going to school. You have decided to play in the park near the school every day.

2. *Mrs. Jones.* You are a third grade teacher. Peter, who is in his fifth year at school, is in your room. He is rarely at school and you have asked the school nurse and the attendance officer to investigate. You have talked with his mother and she has promised to send him to school every day.

3. *Nurse.* Peter's mother says he is sick to his stomach every morning, but she makes him leave for school on time.

4. *Attendance Officer.* Peter has missed ten days in September and fifteen in October. His mother told you that she sends him to school every morning and it isn't her fault if he doesn't get there.

5. *Counselor.* You have talked to Peter and he seemed very shy. He does not verbalize his problems and did not give you any reasons for not attending.

Initial role playing: Mrs. Jones, Attendance Officer, Nurse, and Counselor.

Play 3

Setting: A newly built, suburban, middle-class district with lovely homes and an ultra-modern elementary school.
Characters:

1. *Principal.* You have had a delegation of parents at school demanding that something be done about Mr. Farthing. They have gone to the police, and the incident is under investigation. You have moved Douglas to the vice-principal's class.

2. *Mrs. Henry.* You thought Douglas liked class. He smiled all the time and that had slightly bothered you. He took part in all activities and made average grades. You had never seen him unhappy or uncooperative. The school nurse has informed you that Mr. Farthing is in and out of psychiatric hospitals and that Douglas has had psychiatric counseling for several years. You know nothing about psychiatric patients and are terrified. The children in your class are afraid and have circulated wild stories about Douglas and his father.

3. *Counselor.* The principal has referred Douglas to you for counseling and possible referral to a psychiatric clinic. Douglas, eleven, in fifth grade, smiles at his teacher, Mrs. Henry, all the time. He does all his work and is a good B student. Mrs. Henry was teaching when Douglas came up to her and said, "My Dad is coming here in a few minutes to kill you because you've been so mean to me." Suddenly, the door opened and Douglas' father, Mr. Farthing, appeared with a gun. The children screamed and pandemonium broke loose as everyone ran for the nearest door. When it was over, Mr. Farthing had disappeared and some of the children had run home. Mrs. Henry declared she would not teach Douglas again.

Initial role playing: Mrs. Henry and Counselor.

For Secondary School Counselors

Play 1
Setting: Mary's parents have little money, but have a strong, loving, intellectual homelife. They came from Wales five years ago and have a

bake shop. Both parents are well read and give Mary every encouragement to do well in school.

Characters:

1. *Mary.* You are sixteen, in twelfth grade, and an A student. The sum total of your parents' savings account is $400. They are going to give it to you so that you can go to a private school for secretaries and qualify for a good job. You have proficiency in typing and shorthand and have taken the college preparatory program. You are the best student in your advanced placement chemistry class. You would like to go to college and become a chemist, but there is no money available for you to go to college.

2. *Mrs. Apple.* You are Mary's mother. You want your daughter to be able to earn a good living. You are going to give Mary your life savings to go to secretarial school. College, at $1,000 per semester, has never entered into your plans for Mary.

3. *Counselor.* At the recent college-fair night you noticed that Mary was missing. She has an IQ of 160 and is an outstanding student. She is an accomplished violinist, as well. Mary told you her happy life of study will soon end because she will have to become a secretary. She has to earn a living and help her folks because they will have nothing for their old age without her. You have tried to show her how she could go to college, but she does not believe you.

Initial role playing: Counselor and Mary.

Play 2

Setting: A large high school in an urban area.

Characters:

1. *Joel.* You are seventeen. Your mother died of leukemia when you were thirteen; your father was killed in an accident in the army when you were a baby. This summer your sister, nineteen, died in a car accident. You are living with your grandmother who is eighty-six. Much of the time she is not too well, and she depends on you. You have lost interest in school and feel depressed all the time. You have no desire to work hard and feel there is nothing left in life for you.

2. *Grandmother.* You are worried about Joel. The loss of his sister has been a great blow to both of you. You are not well and are unable to cheer Joel up.

3. *Counselor.* Joel's grandmother phoned and asked you to help Joel. She is worried about him. He has been an average student until this semester.

Initial role playing: Counselor and Joel.

Play 3

Setting: A large high school in an upper-class district.
Characters:

1. *John.* You are seventeen and a high school senior. You have had a very unhappy childhood and have drowned your troubles in drugs and liquor since you were twelve. You have a few acquaintances but no personal friends. You are a member of the high school honor society. Because of your high college entrance exam scores, you have been a semifinalist for three large college scholarships. After the personal interviews, each committee has turned you down because of your inability to communicate with adults and your lack of social skills. You are very unhappy about the results.

2. *Mr. Smith.* You are John's father. You believe all the committees were prejudiced against John because of his ethnic background. You were invited to be part of one of the interviews, and you answered the questions John did not answer. However, you felt the committee didn't like you or your answers. You are very angry with the committees. You are annoyed with your son for not talking up in the interviews.

3. *Counselor.* You agree with the findings of the three interview committees. You believe John has severe emotional problems that need professional care. John comes to you frequently for emotional support. Since the loss of the scholarships, he has come into your office, refused to talk, and stared at you with vacant eyes.

Initial role playing: Counselor and father.

For College Counselors

Play 1

Setting: A junior college in a rural area. Students commute or live on campus. It is a pleasant, friendly place where students and faculty know each other personally.

Characters:

1. *Julie.* You are a sophomore in the Business Department. You intend to transfer to a senior college next year and obtain a degree. You have been unable to study much for the past two months and your grades are suffering. You are twenty and are worried that you may never find a husband. You have never had a steady boyfriend. All the girls in your dorm have boyfriends, but you cannot find anyone. Sometimes friends find a date for you, but you are so shy and awkward you are never asked out again.

2. *Dr. Green.* You are a professor in the junior college. Julie is one of your advisees, and you have found her dates for some of the social functions. This has gone on for two years and now you think Julie should be able to find a date for herself. She is good looking, intelligent, and articulate. You have talked to a counselor because you think Julie needs more help than you can give.

3. *Debra.* You are Julie's roommate. You think Julie is foolish because she thinks she cannot attract dates. You wish you were as beautiful as Julie. You think some fellow will chase Julie some day and marry her. You see no real problem.

4. *Counselor.*

Initial role playing: Counselor and Julie.

Play 2

Setting: A large state university in the Midwest.
Characters:

1. *John.* You are twenty-one and a senior in engineering. You have been accepted into a doctoral program at a major university and have been granted a research assistantship for next year. You realize you do not care if you have a girl friend or not. You have been going to a gay bar, and you feel at home there because everyone is so friendly. You wonder what will happen to your career if you tell everyone how you feel. You have decided to seek professional help.

2. *Mary.* You are John's best friend. He shares his career dreams with you, takes you to class parties, and even makes you cakes to celebrate events in your life. You do not understand his attitudes and wish he would change and be your boyfriend instead of just a friend.

3. *Counselor.* You specialize in helping young people with personal problems. John has sought you out and wants to know the definitions of heterosexual and homosexual.

Initial role playing: Counselor and John.

Play 3

Setting: A small liberal arts school in a rural area.
Characters:
   1. *Mina:* You are twenty-two and a senior in economics. Now that your college life is nearly over, you realize that you do not truly enjoy your major field. You are interested in the subject intellectually but have no idea how it may be used in the world of work. You are afraid that you may be trapped into a lifetime of work you do not enjoy.
   2. *Counselor.* You know little about economics. You have given Mina an interest inventory, and she is strong in business and economics. She is an able student and maintains a B + average.

Initial role playing: Counselor and Mina.

For Career Counseling

Play 1

Setting: A county-sponsored counseling center in an urban area.
Characters:

   1. *Tim.* You are twenty-seven and have given up a career in football due to injuries. You did not make too much money in football, but saved enough money for a downpayment of 50 percent on a house. You own two cars and good furniture. You are married and have two children, two and five years old. You have completed one year of general college courses. You wonder what you should do with the rest of your life. You need a job or profession. You have enough savings to last your family about eighteen months. You have been looking for work, but no one seems to want an injured football player.
   2. *Counselor.* Tim's tests show an intelligence at the 50th percentile. He has about a tenth grade educational background with above-average mechanical aptitude. He has an engaging personality and above-average verbal skills.

Initial role playing: Counselor and Tim.

Play 2

Setting: A private counseling center in a large city.

Characters:

1. *Andrew.* You are forty-two and have worked as an administrative officer in a federal agency since you graduated from college. Your agency has been closed down, and you have been looking for work for three months. You have become very discouraged. You have a wife and three children to support, as well as a mortgage and car payments. Your wife has taken a part-time job as a store clerk and you have been working part-time as a waiter.

2. *Annette.* You are Andrew's wife, and you are very worried about the family's financial situation. You think you may take the management training course offered by the store and go to work full time. You do not like to leave your children but you do not seem to have any alternatives.

3. *Counselor.* Andrew has come to you for help. He seems in low spirits.

Initial role playing: Counselor and Andrew.

Play 3

Setting: A government-sponsored counseling center for persons on county welfare.

Characters:

1. *Mrs. Wheeling.* You are a Native American, thirty-five, and have eight children. You have just had an operation so that you will have no more children. Your oldest child is eighteen, and she has been a scholarship student at the state university for a year. She has just quit school, married, and is living in poverty. You are appalled by her actions and are urging her to go back to school.

2. *May.* You are pregnant and very glad your boyfriend married you. You hated the university and felt ostracized because you are an Indian. You also hated the structure and rigidity of the classes. You are an artist and believe you need personal freedom to create. You think that if your mother believes in the establishment so much, she should go to school and become part of it herself. She is eligible for scholarships because she is an Indian.

3. *Counselor:* Mrs. Wheeling has come to you about May and is also interested in job possibilities for herself.

Initial role playing: Counselor and Mrs. Wheeling.

For Counselors of Those with Emotional Problems

Play 1

Setting: A private counseling center for those with emotional problems.

Characters:

1. *Jane.* You are in your late forties and experiencing "change of life" physical problems. You are feeling most unhappy with yourself and have been taking drugs to make yourself feel better. You were brought up in a religious atmosphere but never understood it. For the past few years you have been reading occult-type literature. This has caused you to have wonderful fantasies about living in different worlds and times. You have been in mental hospitals four times during the past six years. Your husband has divorced you and remarried. He gives you adequate alimony payments.

2. *Jim.* You are Jane's ex-husband and happily remarried. Jane seems to be getting worse, and you believe your daughter, Janet, is being affected by her mother's ideas.

3. *Janet.* You are twenty years old and have a job as a tailor and live with your mother. You are divorced and looking for a steady boyfriend. When life becomes boring, you take drugs.

4. *Counselor.*

Initial role playing: Counselor and Jim.

Play 2

Setting: The counseling center of a large university hospital medical center.

Characters:

1. *Mary Beth.* You are twenty-one, married to a young doctor, and have a one-year-old baby. You have completed two years of college. You were brought up to believe that a woman's "reason for being" was to get married, have children, and be a faithful, loving servant to her husband. You have done everything you believe society requires you to do. You believe your life is over and there is nothing more to look forward to.

2. *Paul.* You are twenty-six and a resident doctor in the hospital. You are completely tired of your marriage and would like to get out of it and marry someone else. Mary Beth cries all the time. She does not keep the house clean or look after the baby properly. She does not attend to your needs, dress properly, or keep herself attractive. All in all, she is a terrible wife, and you can take no more.

3. *Counselor:* Mary Beth has come to you to find out what she can do to stop crying. She says she has cried every day of her marriage, and now she thinks she is sinking into some kind of depression.

Initial role playing: Mary Beth and counselor.

Play 3

Setting: A private counseling center to which hospitals refer patients.

Characters:

1. *Malcolm.* You are forty-two years old, divorced twice, and married for the third time. You have three children by previous marriages. You are in charge of a research laboratory in a chemical corporation. You have been fired from six management positions in your working career because of your inability to get along with other workers. The people in your present lab are circulating a petition to get rid of you because they cannot tolerate your meanness. Because you are worried about your job, you have been screaming at your wife, and she is angry with you.

2. *Mary.* Malcolm fainted while screaming at you. You called an ambulance, and he was rushed to the hospital. He has been there for four days and won't speak to you when you visit. He insists he is dying. The nurses told you that he is the meanest patient they have ever dealt with. You do not understand why he is so angry.

3. *Counselor.* Mary has come to you to find out what she can do. Living with Malcolm is intolerable. She wonders why he screams to the point of fainting.

Initial role playing: Mary and counselor.

For Counselors Working with Criminals

Play 1

Setting: A small counseling office connected with a halfway house in an urban area.

Characters:

1. *Brian.* You are twenty-two and have been in jail several times for theft. You have been on drugs since you were twelve and now your body is showing the results of the abuse. You have just spent two months in the hospital after a jail term, and are living in a halfway house. You work on a construction job during the day and at night have rehabilitative counseling. During the past three days, you have been unable to work due to exhaustion. Your body does not seem to be able to take the heavy lifting required for the job. You realize that for you, going back to your life of thieving would be much easier.

2. *David.* You are a health and physical education specialist who works with persons who have physical liabilities. You find Brian eager to learn, but lacking in stamina and muscle tone.

3. *Counselor.*

Initial role playing: Counselor and Brian.

Play 2

Setting: A counseling office in a large state penitentiary.

Characters:

1. *William.* You are twenty-one and in jail for armed robbery. You are worried about your wife, Jean, age seventeen, and your two

children, six months and two years. They have moved to the town near the jail in order to be near you. They are ineligible for county relief and have no means of support. You have requested an interview with a counselor.

2. *Jean.* You have no family, and William is your main emotional support. You and William have both supported yourselves by theft since you were children. You do not want William to worry about you. You have been in town a week and have stolen enough to get by. The minister in a local church has found you a two-room furnished apartment and brought you a box of food and some baby clothes.

3. *Counselor:* The prison authorities and local townspeople do not want the young wives of prisoners coming to town and expecting to live off the community. You are told to encourage these young women to go back to where they came from.

Initial role playing: Counselor and William.

Play 3

Setting: A small counseling office in a halfway house in a large eastern city.

Characters:

1. *Elise.* You are nineteen and have been in jail several times for soliciting on the streets and for theft. Because of your good behavior, you have been paroled to a halfway house where you have enjoyed the life and the personal interest taken in you by the young counselors. However, you have broken too many of the house rules and are likely to be sent back to the prison farm. You do not believe you could ever learn to live in regular society because the rules seem too restrictive. Yet, you admire the counselors at the halfway house and wish you were like them.

2. *Counselor:* Elise has made excellent progress, but her old life pulls her strongly. She has been placed on one week's probation and told to learn to live within the rules of the house. She seems attracted to your life style and has asked many questions about your values, beliefs, and daily activities.

Initial role playing: Counselor and Elise.

For Family Counselors

Play 1

Setting: A counselor's office in a "safe" house for abused women in a suburban area.

Characters:

1. *Susan.* You are living temporarily in a house for abused women. You do not know what to do. You know you cannot go back to your husband because this time when he beat you up, he also beat up your little girl. You have gone back to him many times before when he hurt you, but you cannot tolerate an injury to your child. You do not know how you can bear to live without the beautiful home, clothing, and material comforts your husband has provided.

2. *Mrs. Mills.* You are Susan's mother, and you are tired of listening to Susan's complaints. You think Susan should accept her husband as he is and be grateful for any mercies she receives.

3. *Ann.* You are Susan's sister. You have sheltered Susan many times. Now your husband is tired of it and doesn't want to see Susan or her husband again. You have a good job and are willing to help her in any way possible.

4. *Counselor.* Susan may stay in the "safe" house for a limited time. She must make decisions about her future.

Initial role playing: Susan and counselor.

Play 2

Setting: A private counseling center.

Characters:

1. *Walter.* You are sixty-two and divorced twice. Your present wife is threatening to leave unless you change your ways. You do not know what you will do if she leaves because you have only your social security check, and it is not enough to maintain you in the way you are accustomed. You have a beautiful home, which is expensive to keep up.

You would also lack companionship, because your grown children avoid you due to the way you treated their mother.

2. *Mary*. You are fifty-eight and have a good pension from your profession, as well as from your first husband's estate. You have told Walter to shape up and get counseling or you will leave him. You feel you are getting too old to take his verbal and physical abuse. You could go and live near your married daughters. You have been married to Walter for nine years.

3. *Counselor.*

Initial role playing: Counselor and Walter.

Play 3

Setting: A women's counseling center in a small town.

Characters:

1. *Viola*. You are thirty-seven. Your husband left you with three children—ages three, seven, and fourteen—and no means of support. You are on county welfare and manage fairly well, although at times your family lacks adequate meals. Your church pays tuition and school lunches to a parochial school, and you are glad the children are getting a good education. Your fourteen-year-old son spends weekends with his father, is on drugs, and has rejected the values of the parochial school to which he is being sent. You are upset because church people are giving money for your son's education and he is wasting the opportunity.

Your seven-year-old daughter is thin and listless, lacking in energy, and having difficulty in school. You do not know what to do for her. You do not have the means to give her an adequate diet and proper health care.

You are 5 feet, 6 inches tall, weigh 100 pounds, and are ill much of the time.

2. *Counselor*. This family has been referred to you by the pastor of the parochial school. Because the son is on drugs, he has been dropped from the school.

Initial role playing: Counselor and pastor of the church that supports the parochial school.

For Counselors Working with the Elderly

Play 1

Setting: A counseling center in a large senior citizens' complex where people come to swim, bowl, play tennis and golf, and take part in a wide range of activities.

Characters:

1.   *Agnes.* You are sixty-two years of age and your husband is seventy. He has been very ill, and you have spent the past two years nursing him. You are physically and emotionally drained. He is now much better and has been going on outings with the senior citizens and having a wonderful time. You do not consider yourself a senior citizen and do not want to go out with so many old people.

2.   *Aaron.* You are Agnes' husband. You wish she would come with you to the senior citizens' outings. Everyone has a grand time. You know that Agnes is very unhappy, but you do not know what to do for her.

3.   *Debra.* You are Agnes' daughter. Until six months ago, you and your son had been living with your parents. You have remarried and your mother is trying to persuade your ten-year-old son to come back and live with her. You are beginning a new life and wish your mother would let you go. You have offered to drive your mother to the senior citizens' center, but she won't go.

4.   *Counselor.* Debra has come to you because she is worried about her mother's unhappiness.

Initial role playing: Debra and counselor.

Play 2

Setting: A counseling center in a wealthy retirement community in Florida.

Characters:

1.   *Emma.* You are eighty-two and in excellent health. You are wealthy because your two husbands were fine businessmen. You were a

beauty queen when young, and men still find you attractive. You have been dating a retired school principal who taught your children years ago. He wants to marry you; you do not know what to do.

2. *Joanne.* You are Emma's daughter. You find your mother's amorous escapades amusing but foolish at her age. You cannot understand why she is not content with her large family of grandchildren and great grandchildren.

3. *Michael.* You want to marry Emma. You love her and have known her for sixty years. Emma tells you she is too old to marry and that you should be content to be her friend.

4. *Counselor.*

Initial role playing: Counselor and Michael.

Play 3

Setting: A counseling office in a community senior citizens' center.
Characters:

1. *James.* You are seventy-five, widowed, and live by yourself in your own home. You realize that in the next few years you will find housekeeping beyond your physical and emotional powers to handle. To prepare for this eventuality, you have legally drawn up a will and provided for care for yourself in case of incapacity. You have bought a condominium apartment in a retirement community four hundred miles away. You intended, when you bought it, to move there when you were seventy-five. Now you want to stay where you are. You are still vigorous and healthy and do not want to move away from all your friends.

2. *Peter.* You are James' son. You wish your father would move to the beautiful retirement estate he has bought. He would be much closer to you, and you could keep an eye on him. He would also be able to see his grandchildren more often.

3. *Joe.* You are widowed, retired, and live down the street from James. You and James play cards every day, take the bus to the senior citizens' center, and also help each other when needed. You do not know what you would do if James moved away.

4. *Counselor.*

Initial role playing: Counselor and Peter.

BIBLIOGRAPHY

Alberti, R. E., and M. A. Emmons. *Your Perfect Right: A Guide to Assertive Behavior.* San Luis Obispo, Cal.: Impact Press, 1970.

Atkinson, Donald R., and George Morten. *Counseling American Minorities: A Cross Cultural Perspective.* Dubuque, Iowa: Wm. C. Brown, 1979.

Axline, Virginia. *Play Therapy.* New York: Ballantine Books, 1969.

Bandura, A. *Principles of Behavior Modification.* New York: Holt, Rinehart and Winston, 1969.

Beek, Carlton E. *Philosophical Guidelines for Counseling.* Dubuque, Iowa: Wm. C. Brown, 1966.

Bennett, Lawrence A., and Thomas S. Rosenbaum. *Counseling in Correctional Environments.* New Vistas in Counseling Series, Vol. 6. New York: Human Sciences Press, 1978.

Berne, Eric. *Games People Play.* New York: Grove Press, 1964.

Berne, Eric. *What Do You Say After You Say Hello?* New York: Grove Press, 1972.

Bessell, Robert. *Interviewing and Counseling.* Batsford, England: David and Charles, 1976.

Blackham, Garth J., and Adolph Silberman. *Modification of Child Behavior.* Belmont, Calif.: Wadsworth, 1971.

Bogardus, E. S. "Measuring Social Distance." *Journal of Applied Sociology,* 9 (1925).

Borck, Leslie E., and Stephen B. Fawcett. *Learning Counseling and Problem-Solving Skills.* New York: Haworth Press, 1981.

The Buckley Amendment/The Family Educational Rights and Privacy Act of 1974, and the Educational Amendments Act of 1974. Washington, D.C.: Federal Register.

Brown-Azarowicz, Marjory. *Individual and Group Assessment Procedures in Reading for grades 4-7.* Washington, D.C.: University Press of America, 1982.

Burgum, T., and S. Anderson. *The Counselor and the Law.* Falls Church, Va.: APGA Press, 1975.

Bryan, Reddick. *Effective Writing Style.* New York: Richard Prosen Press, 1976.

Christiansen, Harley D. *Ethics in Counseling: Problem Situations.* Tucson: University of Arizona Press, 1972.

The Code of Ethics. Washington, D.C.: National Education Association, 1974.

Corey, Gerald, et al. *Professional and Ethical Issues in Counseling and Psychotherapy.* Monterey, Cal.: Brooks-Cole, 1979.

Cormier, William H., and Louise S. Cormier. *Interviewing Strategies for Helpers.* Monterey, Cal.: Brooks-Cole, 1979.

Cormier, William H. and Louise S. Cormier. *Behavioral Counseling: Initial Procedures for Individual and Group Strategies.* Boston, Mass.: Houghton Mifflin, 1975.

Corsini, Raymond J., et al. *Current Psychotherapies.* Itasca, Ill.: Peacock, 1979.

Cull, John G. and Richard E. Hardy. *Counseling Strategies with Special Populations.* Springfield, Ill.: C. C. Thomas, 1975.

Cunningham, Ruth. *Understanding Group Behavior of Boys and Girls.* New York: Bureau of Publications, Teachers' College, Columbia University, 1951.

Downing, Lester N. *Counseling Theories and Techniques: Summarized and Critiqued.* Chicago, Ill.: Nelson-Hall, 1975.

"Ethical Principles of Psychologists." *American Psychologist,* 36, no. 6 (June 1981).

Ethical Standards. Falls Church, Va.: American Personnel and Guidance Association, 1981.

Fischer, Louis, and David Schimmel. *The Rights of Students and Teachers.* New York: Harper and Row, 1982.

Frey, David H., and Frederick E. Heslet. *Existential Theory for Counselors.* Boston, Mass.: Houghton Mifflin, 1975.

Gambrill, E. *Behavior Modification: Handbook of Assessment Intervention and Evaluation.* San Francisco, Cal.: Jossey-Bass, 1977.

Gendlin, E. J. *Experiencing and the Creation of Meaning.* New York: Free Press of Glencoe, 1962.

Glasser, William. *Reality Therapy.* New York: Harper and Row, 1965.

Glasser, William. *Schools Without Failure.* New York: Harper and Row, 1969.

"Guidelines on Employment Selection Procedures." *Federal Register,* 35, no. 149 (Aug. 1, 1970), 12333–36.

Hansen, James C., Richard R. Stevic, and Richard W. Warner, Jr. *Counseling Theory and Process.* Boston, Mass: Allyn and Bacon, 1977.

Harris, Thomas. *I'm OK—You're OK: A Practical Guide to Transactional Analysis.* New York: Harper and Row, 1969.

Heidegger, Martin. *Being and Time.* New York: Harper and Row, 1962.

Hoffman, John C. *Ethical Confrontation in Counseling.* Chicago, Ill.: University of Chicago Press, 1981.

Holscher, H. *How to Organize and Write a Technical Report.* Paterson, N.J.: Littlefield, Adams, 1965.

Huckens, Wesley. *Ethical and Legal Considerations in Guidance.* Boston, Mass.: Houghton Mifflin, 1968.

Jackson, K. F. *The Art of Solving Problems.* New York: St. Martin's Press, 1975.

Jongeward, Dorothy, and Muriel James. *Winning with People.* Menlo Park, Cal.: Addison-Wesley, 1973.

Keefe, Frances J., Steven A. Kopel, and Steven B. Gordon. *A Practical Guide to Behavioral Assessment.* New York: Springer, 1978.

Kiley, M. A. *Personal and Interpersonal Appraisal Techniques.* Springfield, Ill.: C. C. Thomas, 1975.

Klein, M. H., P. L. Mathiew, D. J. Keesler, and E. T. Gendlin. *The Experiencing Scale Manual.* Madison: University of Wisconsin Press, 1970.

Kock, S., ed. *Psychology: A Study of Science. Vol. III: Formulations of the Person and the Social Content.* New York: McGraw-Hill 1959.

Meyer, James B., and Joyce K. Meyer. *Counseling Psychology.* Boston, Mass.: Allyn and Bacon, 1975.

Nygaard, Joseph M. *The Counselor and Student: Legal Rights.* Boston, Mass.: Houghton Mifflin, 1973.

Okun, Barbara F. *Effective Helping: Interviewing and Counseling Techniques.* Monterey, Cal.: Brooks-Cole, 1981.

Osipow, Samuel H., et al. *A Survey of Counseling Methods.* Homewood, Ill.: Dorsey, 1980.

Patterson, C. H. *Theories of Counseling and Psychotherapy.* New York: Harper and Row, 1966.

Pedersen, Paul B., et al., eds. *Counseling Across Cultures.* Honolulu, University Press of Hawaii, 1981.

Ponzo, Zander. "Integrating Techniques from Five Counseling Theories." *Personnel and Guidance Journal,* 54, no. 8 (April 1976).

Pulveno, Charles J., and Nicholas Colangelo. *Counseling for the Growing Years: Sixty-five and Over.* Minneapolis, Minn.: Educational Media Corp., 1980.

Reddick, Bryan. *Effective Writing Style.* New York: Richard Prosen Press, 1976.

Rogers, Carl R. *Client-Centered Therapy.* Boston, Mass.: Houghton Mifflin, 1951.

Rogers, Carl R. *On Becoming a Person.* Boston, Mass.: Houghton Mifflin, 1961.

Rogers, Carl R. *Carl Rogers on Personal Power.* New York: Delacorte Press, 1977.

Sahakian, William S., ed. *Psychotherapy and Counseling.* Chicago, Ill.: Rand McNally, 1976.

Schertzer, Bruce, and James D. Linden. *Fundamentals of Individual Appraisal: Assessment Techniques for Counselors.* Boston, Mass.: Houghton Mifflin, 1978.

Schimmel, David, and Louis Fisher. *The Civil Rights of Students.* New York: Harper and Row, 1975.

Schueberger, James M. and David G. Watterson. *Using Tests and Other Information in Counseling: A Decision Model for Practitioners.* Champaign, Ill.: Institute of Personality and Ability, 1977.

Skoholt, Thomas. "Guided Fantasy in Career Counseling." *Personnel and Guidance Journal,* 52, no. 10 (June 1974).

Test Service Bulletin No. 54, Dec. 1959, The Psychological Corp.

Test Service Bulletin No. 36, Aug. 1948, The Psychological Corp.

The Testing Digest. New York: The Committee for Fair and Open Testing, 1980.

Van Hoose, William H., and Louis, V. Paradise. *Ethics in Counseling and Psychotherapy: Perspectives on Issues & Decision-Making.* Cranston, R.I.: Carroll Press, 1979.

White, Earl E. and Hazel I. Smith. *A Guide to Behavior Modification.* Palo Alto, Cal.: Peek Publications, 1973.

Index